MINT

Johnny Acton

THINK
BOOKS

First published 2007 by Think Books
an imprint of Pan Macmillan Ltd
Pan Macmillan, 20 New Wharf Road, London N1 9RR
Basingstoke and Oxford
Associated companies throughout the world
www.panmacmillan.com
www.think-books.com

ISBN: 978-1-84525-047-8
Text Copyright: Pan Macmillan Ltd 2007
Design Copyright: Think Publishing

Author: Johnny Acton
Commissioning editor: Emma Jones
Assistant editor: Tania Adams
Sub editors: Rica Dearman, Caitlin Mackesy Davies and Marion Thompson
Designers: Lou Millward, Dom Scott
Publisher: Mark Searle

1 3 5 7 9 8 6 4 2

A CIP catalogue record for this book is available from the British Library.

Printed and bound in England by Butler and Tanner

Visit www.panmacmillan.com to read more about all our books and to buy
them. You will also find features, author interviews and news of any
author events, and you can sign up for e-newsletters so that you're
always first to hear about our new releases.

A mark, a yen, a buck or a pound
Is all that makes the world go round
That clinking, clanking sound
Can make the world go round

– Cabaret

THANKS

The author would like to thank his wife Percy (as usual), his father (ditto), Frank Gillespie (for rummaging through dustbins in southern Spain looking for useful news stories), Anand Thyagarajan (for a lead on the Vedic Raam), Joe Corbett (for an unprintable story about what two cigarettes could buy in Germany immediately after World War II) and everyone who has listened to him yammer on about money during the writing of this book.

With special thanks to Jes Stanfield who first suggested the concept of this book.

AUTHOR'S NOTE

This book makes no pretence at being exhaustive. If it did, it would be the size of several telephone directories. Instead, it seeks to give some vital background at the start and then to roam joyously among some of the world's more interesting banknotes and coins in the A-Z section. The currencies of some huge, important countries have been omitted entirely. If this applies to your homeland or place of origin, forgive me. Maybe it will be put right in a subsequent volume. In the meantime, just enjoy.

CONTENTS

INTRODUCTION

GOATS AND AXES: THE TROUBLE WITH BARTER

Before the invention of money, the only way to trade goods was via barter. If you had a spare goat but wanted a big pile of wheat, you had to find someone in the reverse position. This would have been fine in a community where the only possessions were wheat and goats, but once you threw a few more items into the mix the limitations of the barter system became glaringly obvious.

First, there was the problem of matching up desires. What if the person with the wheat was only interested in swapping it for hand axes? It could be a long time before the first man found an axe-rich individual in desperate need of a goat. In the meantime, he might starve.

Second, what if the wheat man did want a goat, but not until his daughter's wedding in three months' time? Had they been able to read and write, the protagonists could have drawn up a contract, but at this stage there were no literate societies. Even if there had been, a system relying on written records of who owed what to whom would have become hopelessly unwieldy once there was a reasonable amount of trade going on. As it was, the parties to the deal would have had to rely on memory. This was open to abuse ('What are you talking about? I never said I'd give you a whole goat!') and still more liable to become overtaxed ('If Ug owes Stig seven axes, Stig owes Rok four clubs and Rok owes Ug two goats, how many bear hides does Stig owe Yed?'). And there was always the risk that the poor old goat might turn up its toes before the wedding day.

THE BIRTH OF MONEY

One day, an anonymous Neolithic farmer came up with an ingenious solution. Why not settle on something that everyone agreed was worth having? This could then be used to buy goats, axes, clubs and all the rest of it. The dollar bill signs flashed in the proto-economist's mind. Eventually his big idea would become known as 'money'.

After a period of trial and error, it became apparent that candidates for this exciting new function had to have certain characteristics. They needed to be:

♦ Scarce – Ordinary pebbles would be useless as a form of money, at least in most places. They are just too easy to obtain. It wouldn't seem right to trade the goat you had lovingly reared for years for a handful of stones that the buyer could simply pick off the ground.

♦ Difficult to fake – This is related to the scarcity imperative. A monetary system based on pieces of paper with simple crosses on them would be doomed to failure. If people could literally make money with the minimum of effort, the temptation would be hard to resist. The result would be galloping inflation and a total loss of confidence in the currency.

♦ Portable – You can certainly trade items like houses and mountains, but taking them to the local market is not really practical. OK, the Yap islanders did have stone 'coins' that weighed several tons (see page 142), but they also had little ones for everyday transactions.

♦ Durable – A commodity like salt might seem a potential goer as a currency, but you would be rapidly disabused of this idea if you left your supply out in the rain.

♦ Easily divisible – Imagine a society where the only form of money was the $100 bill. Although this wouldn't be a problem with relatively large transactions, it would be a mighty headache if you just wanted a box of matches. To work efficiently, units of currency need to be divisible into smaller units. For this reason, live goats are not a viable option.

♦ Desirable – Nowadays we are all delighted to receive pieces of paper adorned with the right symbols, but this is only because of the symbolic value they have acquired through long and complex chains of events. An early farmer would have been distinctly underwhelmed to be handed a wad of £50 notes. To part with his goods, he would have needed to be given items that were directly exciting in themselves. Shiny, pretty or inherently useful things would have come to mind.

With these criteria in mind, or perhaps more likely operating unconsciously, our ancestors developed the first primitive forms of money. Cowrie shells were a popular early choice, as were precious or semi-precious stones and metals. The latter became increasingly important in the payment of tribute, which the empires that were now beginning to form started to extract from their subject territories. Such forms of what can loosely be described as cash are technically known as 'commodity money'.

PRIMITIVE BANKS

At this stage there were no coins. Instead, the value of metal was judged by its weight. The legacy of this can be seen in words such as the English 'spend', which is derived from the Latin verb *expendere*, meaning 'to weigh'. Before coins (and later banknotes) could come into existence, the institution of banking had to be invented. This order of events may seem surprising, but if you think about it, notes and coins need pre-existing bureaucratic structures to give them their validity. As we shall see, one of their crucial features until relatively recently was the 'promise to pay the bearer' clause. The holder had to have confidence that there were institutions that would exchange these symbolic forms of money for the commodity that underpinned them (often gold), or at least that they would do so in theory.

The first banking institutions were royal palaces, temples and state warehouses in Mesopotamia and Egypt. Because they were well guarded, these places were considered ideal for the storage of grain and other commodities. Those making deposits would be issued with receipts, which could then be used to conduct transactions with other parties. Written on clay tablets or papyrus, they can be regarded as the forerunners of today's transferable cheques and banknotes. As the practice of using such receipts to make purchases caught on, private banking houses began to appear. They are mentioned (and regulated) in the Babylonian Code of Hammurabi (c.1,760BC).

EARLY COINS

The scene was almost set for the invention of coins. In the meantime, the Chinese came up with a couple of interesting intermediate stages between commodity money and true coinage. In about 1,000BC, after at least two centuries of conducting transactions with the genuine articles, they started using bronze and copper models of cowrie shells. Then, around the eighth century BC, 'spade' and 'knife' monies came into vogue. These were miniaturised versions of agricultural implements that were too small to be of practical use, but gave nods to items that were. Nevertheless, they came in standardised weights and tended to be marked by the issuing authority.

The world's first true coins are widely believed to have been minted in Lydia in Asia Minor around 640BC (see 'Oldest Coin' entry). They were made of an alloy of gold and silver called electrum and were probably made to guarantee the purity of the constituent metal. The design – a roaring lion's head symbolising the ruling Mermnad dynasty – was stamped on one side only. This was a result of the primitive method of manufacture. Blank pieces of electrum were placed over dies and blows were struck against their reverses. At first such 'hammer marks' were plain, but when the practice of minting coins spread to other parts of the Greek-speaking world they began to incorporate the badges of the issuing cities. In time, the Persians and other ancient peoples started to produce coins of their own.

THE RISE OF PAPER MONEY

The next phase in the evolution of currency was the invention of paper money. The first banknotes were issued in China during the reign of Emperor Hien Tsung (AD806-821), but not as a result of any great financial insight. The sole reason for their introduction was an acute copper shortage that precluded the striking of new coins. Eventually, China got carried away with the ease of producing this new form of cash. Too much of it was printed and this led to inflation. In 1455, the Chinese abandoned the use of paper money and did not return to it for several centuries.

The Chinese experience was repeated when Sweden became the first European nation to experiment with paper money. In 1661, a banker named Johan Palmstruch began to issue credit notes that could be exchanged at his Stockholm bank for stated numbers of silver coins. Unfortunately for Palmstruch, who had consulted the Swedish government before launching the scheme, he got carried away with his licence to print money. He issued more notes than his bank had silver deposits to redeem, and in 1668 was prosecuted for fraud. He was initially sentenced to death, but the penalty was later commuted to imprisonment.

Despite the less than glorious outcomes to these early trials of paper money, the tide of history was firmly on the side of the new form of currency. As economic activity increased in Europe, it became apparent that the money supply needed to be expanded beyond the limits imposed by holdings of precious metals. This recognition led to the establishment of the first national central banks. People were much more likely to trust notes backed by government reserves than those issued by private institutions. They even proved willing to accept temporary governmental bans on the redemption of banknotes for silver, as happened in Britain during the 'Restriction Period' of 1797 to 1821 (see 'Goldsmiths, banking and banknotes' on page 26).

THE GOLD STANDARD

Entrusting the issue of banknotes to one central authority effectively removed the danger of bankruptcy, but it did raise the spectre of inflation. This would happen if a central bank printed too much money. (To understand this, imagine you were an egg seller and everyone suddenly had twice as much cash. You would feel foolish, not to say cheated, if you continued to sell your eggs at the old price.) It was the risk of inflation, among other factors, that propelled governments into joining the Gold Standard, a measure that in some ways harked back to the days when all money really was made of precious metal.

The Gold Standard was a mechanism that fixed the values of the coins and banknotes of participating nations in terms of specified quantities of gold. The Standard operated both domestically and internationally. On the domestic front, it forestalled inflation by ensuring that the money supply remained relatively constant. There were two reasons for this. First, the introduction of significant quantities of new gold into the system was rare. When it did happen, as in the US following the California gold rush (1848-1864), the result was significant inflation. Second, a crucial aspect of the Gold Standard was that non-gold forms of money, such as notes and bank deposits, could be freely converted into gold and vice versa. This rendered the chances of a run on either form of money pointless and therefore close to zero.

In the international sphere, the Gold Standard had the effect of fixing exchange rates between the nations involved. If the US set the price of gold at $20.67 per ounce, for example, as it did from 1834 until 1933, and the UK set it at three pounds 17 shillings and 10.5 pence, as it did from 1844 until 1931 (apart from a period after World War I), an exchange rate of $4.867 dollars to the pound necessarily followed. The benefits of fixed exchange rates included stability and a balancing of prices between subscribing nations. If the UK, for example, made a technological breakthrough that increased economic output, its prices would fall. (There was little alternative so long as the money supply was constant.)

Assuming US prices stayed the same, this would make UK products more attractive from an American perspective, and American products less attractive to the UK. The upshot would be that gold – ie, the stuff in which payments were made – would flow out of the US and into Britain. As the money supply/ amount of gold in Britain had now increased, its prices would rise. At the same time, US prices would fall in line with the nation's own money supply. Hey presto, everyone ended up more or less where they had been in the first place and price stability was restored.

The Gold Standard worked very well so long as everyone played nicely. In the US, for example, inflation between 1880 and 1914 averaged a mere 0.1% per year. The trouble was that many of the participating nations were inclined to cheat, particularly when the going got tough. When World War I broke out in 1914, the countries involved threw their rule books out of the window. They started printing money to finance their war efforts and the Gold Standard broke down. It was reinstated in modified form in 1925, but collapsed again due to instability caused by the Great Depression. In 1931, Britain left the Gold Standard as a result of massive outflows of gold from the nation's coffers.

The successor to the Gold Standard was the Bretton Woods system, named after the New Hampshire resort where the World War II Allies thrashed out the details in 1944. Once again, exchange rates were fixed (within a margin of 1%), but the key feature was that all participating nations apart from the US were allowed to settle their debts in US dollars. The US promised to redeem the dollar holdings of other countries for gold at a fixed rate of $35 per ounce. Unfortunately, this offer was taken up to the extent that the US started running out of gold, which placed the entire system in jeopardy. In 1971, President Nixon announced that the US would no longer be paying out gold for dollars. For the Gold Standard, this was the final nail in the coffin.

FIAT MONEY

Since 1971, the world economy has largely run on a system of floating exchange rates, with gold-backed currency replaced by what is called 'fiat money'. This is money that has no intrinsic value and obtains its worth entirely on the basis of governmental decree. ('This piece of paper can be used to pay debts because we say it can.') The use of fiat money obviously places a greater responsibility on governments than they had in the days when currency had to be backed by precious metals. Print too much of it and you end up in a right mess…

CREDIT CARDS, DEBIT CARDS AND E-MONEY

The technological revolution of the late twentieth century has spawned all sorts of alternatives to cash and cheques. However, as this is primarily a book about banknotes and coins, let us move swiftly on.

THE BIG THREE: £, $ AND €

THE POUND

The history of British currency is pretty tortuous as it reflects the complex history of the British Isles. England and Wales have effectively shared a currency since the Norman Conquest. The medieval Scottish currency system mimicked its English equivalent, but the two currencies gradually drifted apart in value. The Act of Union brought them back into line in 1707, since when they have had identical values, but the Scots, unlike the Welsh, have continued to print their own banknotes. (They are actually 'promissory notes', but let's not go there in this section.) The historical relationship between English and Irish currency is, if anything, even more complicated. The two went in and out of synchronicity for hundreds of years before uniting in 1826 and parting for good in 1979. Northern Ireland, however, still uses the UK pound, though it prints its own notes. And don't get me started on the Channel Islands, the Isle of Man, Gibraltar, the Falklands and St Helena. The first two have what are known as 'regional issues' of sterling while the others issue currencies that are tied to sterling. More information about the notes and coins of some of these territories can be found in the relevant sections. In the meantime, consider what follows to always refer to England and Wales, usually to refer to England and Scotland, sometimes to refer to England and Northern Ireland, and occasionally to refer to England and the whole of Ireland (prior to its division)!

LSD

The English and Welsh money system prior to decimalisation in 1971 had nothing to do with lysergic acid, but it does now seem a little psychedelic. Amounts were expressed in pounds, shillings and pence (singular 'penny'), for which the respective symbols were an 'L' with a crossbar through it (from the Latin *libra*, meaning a pound as a unit of mass), a lower case 's' (standing for a Roman coin called a *sestertius*) and a 'd' (an abbreviation for another Roman coin, the *denarius*). Two pounds, five shillings and eight pennies, for example, was written as £2 5s 8d, or alternatively as £2/5/8. There were 12 pennies to a shilling, 20 shillings to a pound and therefore 240 pennies to a pound. The advantage of this system (there was one!) was that 12 and 240 were more amenable to division than 10 and 100. You could, for example, split the old pound into three equal packages of 6s 8d, whereas 33^1/$_3$p is an impossibility coinage-wise.

It will come as no surprise that nobody thought up this convoluted system in one stroke. Instead, it gradually evolved. Prior to the late fifteenth century, pounds and shillings were merely accounting terms. Another was the mark, which was worth 160 pence or $^2/_3$ of a pound. The only coins in circulation were fractions and multiples of pennies or the good old penny itself. Then, in 1489, Henry VII revolutionised the monetary system by ordering coins to be struck in denominations of pounds and shillings. (Actually, he ordered them to be minted in pounds and testoons, but you're probably confused enough already. It came to the same thing: a testoon was worth 12 pence, just like the shilling. Its name was changed to the 'modern' version in 1551.)

For many centuries, the value of a coin was determined by the amount of silver or gold it contained. As the prices of these metals changed over time, three things could happen to coins of a given denomination. First, the size in which they were minted could be changed. Second, the percentage of precious metal in the alloy of which they were made could be altered, as happened to silver coins during the reign of Edward VI (1547-1553). Finally, coins could find themselves worth more or less than their face values. In 1526, for instance, Henry VIII increased the value of gold coins in circulation by 10%.

Here is a fairly exhaustive table of English coins and their values for the period from 959 to decimalisation, in order of value. Hold on to your hats…

Farthing (¼ penny) .... withdrawn 1960. Originally made by cutting pennies into quarters ('fourthings'). First minted in 1279

Half penny/Ha'penny (½ penny) ....withdrawn 1969. Originally made by cutting pennies into halves. First minted in 1279

Three farthing (¾ penny) .... minted under Elizabeth I (1558-1603)

Penny (1 penny) ... prior to 1279, this was the only coin in regular circulation

Half groat (2 pence) .... introduced c.1352

Twopence (2 pence) ....replaced half groat in 1660

Threepence (3 pence) .... first minted in 1551

Groat (4 pence) ....first minted in 1279. Discontinued 1856

Fourpence (4 pence) ....replaced groat in 1660

Sixpence (6 pence) .... first minted in 1551

Ninepence (9 pence) ....minted 1811 to 1816

Testoon (12 pence/1s) ....introduced in 1489

Shilling (12 pence/1s) ....replaced the testoon in 1551

Helm (18 pence/1s 6d) ....introduced in 1344

Eighteen pence (18 pence/1s 6d) ....minted 1811 to 1816

Gold penny (20 pence/1s 8d) .... briefly minted during the 1250s

Quarter noble (20 pence/1s 8d) .... fourteenth century

Florin, new (24 pence/2s) .... first minted in 1849

Quarter ryal (30 pence/2s 6d) .... fifteenth century

Half crown (30 pence/2s 6d) ....introduced in 1526

Leopard (36 pence/3s) ....introduced in 1344

Three shilling (36 pence/3s) ....minted 1811 to 1816

Half noble (40 pence/3s 4d) .... fourteenth century

Half angel (40 pence/3s 4d) .... issued under Henry VII (1485-1507)

Thistle crown (48 pence/4s) ....issued under James I (1603-1625)

Double florin (48 pence/4s) .... minted 1887 to 1890 to commemorate Queen Victoria's Golden Jubilee

Crown of the rose (54 pence/4s 6d) ....introduced by Henry VIII in 1526

Dollar*** (57 pence/4s 9d) .... emergency issue 1804

Half ryal (60 pence/5s) .... fifteenth century

Crown, of the double rose (60 pence/5s) ....introduced in 1526

Quarter laurel (60 pence/5s) ....minted 1619 to 1625

Bank of England dollar*** (60 pence/5s) ....issued in 1804

Florin, old (72 pence/6s) ....introduced in 1344

Noble (80 pence/6s 8d) .... fourteenth century

Angel (80 pence/6s 8d) 1465

George noble (80 pence/6s 8d) .... first minted in 1526

Third guinea (84 pence/7s) ....minted 1797 to 1812

Ryal (120 pence/10s) 1465

Half Sovereign* (120 pence/10s) .... first minted in 1526

Half laurel (120 pence/10s) .... minted 1619 to 1625

Double crown (120 pence/10s) .... issued under Charles I (1625-1649), last minted in 1662

Half guinea** (126 pence/10s 6d) ......first minted in 1663, withdrawn 1821

Spur ryal (180 pence/15s) ....issued under James I

Sovereign (240 pence/20s/£1) ....introduced in 1489

Pound (240 pence/20s/£1) ....became basic monetary unit in 1816

Unite (240 pence/20s/£1) .... issued in 1604 to commemorate union with Scotland

Laurel (240 pence/20s/£1) .... replaced the Unite (1619-1625)

Guinea** (252 pence/21s/£1 1s) .... first minted in 1663, withdrawn 1821

Fine sovereign (360 pence/30s/£1 10s) ....minted in 1551

Rose ryal (360 pence/30s/£1 10s) .... first minted in 1604

Two guineas** (504 pence/42s/£2 2s) .... first minted in 1663

Five guineas** (1,260 pence/105s/£5 5s) .... first minted in 1663

Note on the pound: at some defining moment in Anglo-Saxon times, if you had been lucky enough to own 240 silver pennies you would literally have had a pound of silver. This is believed to be the ultimate origin of the 240d to £1 equation.

---

* The half sovereign was actually worth 132 pence/11s shortly after its introduction because Henry VIII increased the value of gold coins by 10%. This temporarily made the half angel worth 44 pence/3s 8d, the angel worth 88 pence/7s 4d and the sovereign worth 264 pence/22s. In 1551, the sovereign reverted to its 'normal' value of 240 pence/20s, the half sovereign to 120 pence/10s, and so on.

** The guinea was initially worth 20s but its value increased as the price of gold rose. In 1694 it reached a high of 30s. In 1717 the value of the guinea was fixed at 21s. For more information on the guinea, see page 34.

*** The dollar was adopted as an emergency measure in 1804 due to an acute shortage of gold caused by the Napoleonic Wars. At first, dollars were made by counter-striking Spanish American 'pieces of eight' (eight-real coins), or occasionally French ecus or American dollars. These adapted coins, valued at 4s 9d, proved easy to forge. As a result, the Bank of England began to use the foreign coins to strike completely new 'dollars', valued at 5s.

GOLDSMITHS, BANKING AND BANKNOTES

Prior to the Stuart era, England's gold and silver reserves were stored in the Tower of London. When Charles I helped himself to the tune of £130,000, the country's businessmen decided it would be better to stash their loot elsewhere. They turned to London's goldsmiths, the one class of people that could be relied upon to have safe safes.

In time, two practices developed that would revolutionise the world of money. The first was that customers started issuing written instructions to their goldsmiths to make payments to third parties. These were the original cheques. Secondly, the receipts that the goldsmiths gave those who made deposits with them began to take on lives of their own. Once the words 'or the bearer' were inserted after the names of depositors, they became transferable, just like the ancient temple receipts mentioned in the introduction to this book. Since it was much easier to carry pieces of paper around than, say, £100 in gold coins, people gradually stopped using precious metals to conduct their transactions and used the 'banknotes' that represented them instead, particularly where large amounts were concerned.

The earliest 'official' English banknotes were issued in 1694 by the newly formed Bank of England, which had been set up to underwrite the costs of William III's war against France. Like the goldsmiths' receipts, the notes included a clause in which the Bank's chief cashier 'promise(d) to pay the bearer the sum of X on demand'. In other words, anyone in possession of such a note could go to the Bank and redeem it for gold or coinage.

The earliest Bank of England notes were handwritten on paper and signed by one of the cashiers. They were made out for the precise sums deposited, eg £28 11s 6d. If the owner withdrew only part of the specified sum, the value of the note would be adjusted by hand. The practice of issuing fixed denomination notes emerged in stages.

In 1725, the Bank started printing notes with the '£' sign and first digit of the value already in place, but the cashier still had to sign the note, number it, fill in the amount and write in the name of the payee. Ready-made £10 notes were first issued in 1759 and their £5 equivalents in 1793, but a cashier still had to sign them and write in the names of the payees. They were not relieved of this duty until 1855.

At first, Bank of England notes were not popular with the general public as people outside the business community had difficulty trusting them. This problem was exacerbated in 1695 when Daniel Perrismore was fined for forging 60 £100 notes, an enormous sum at the time. The authorities subsequently introduced the death penalty to deter would-be forgers, but there was still widespread reluctance to accept paper money. In 1797, however, the public was given little option in the matter. In response to a series of runs on its gold reserves caused by concerns about the war against Napoleon, the Bank of England took drastic steps. In what was known as the Restriction Period, it stopped paying out gold in exchange for its banknotes and ceased minting gold coins with a value above half a guinea. To replace them, it printed the first £1 and £2 notes. They were issued on 26 February 1797.

This first phase of widespread banknote use came to an end in 1817, when the Bank of England felt able to recommence the production of higher value gold coins. This time, however, they were minted in denominations of pounds rather than guineas. But the door to the general acceptance of banknotes was now open, and in 1833 Bank of England notes worth £5 and above were made legal tender. (Notes worth £10, £20, £50, £100, £500 and even £1,000 were also issued at this time.) The purpose of this move was to protect the Bank's bullion reserves in the event of a crisis. People were still theoretically entitled to redeem banknotes for gold, but if the notes were legal tender they would have little reason to bother.

Interestingly, at this stage the Bank had no monopoly on the printing of notes. The first move in this direction was the 1844 Bank Charter Act, which forbade the establishment of new banks entitled to issue notes and prevented those that already did so from expanding their issues. The Act also stipulated that any issuing bank that merged with a non-issuing bank would lose its rights to print notes. These measures eventually led to the death of the private banknote in England. The last ones were issued by Fox, Fowler & Co of Somerset in 1921.

OLD WHITE FIVER

Until comparatively recently, English banknotes were dull affairs printed in black ink on white paper. The only decorations were a figure of Britannia in a small oval vignette and, from 1855, the words 'Bank of England' in an elaborate typeface. The first coloured English banknotes were the (brown) 10 shilling and (green) £1 issued by the Bank of England in 1928. (Notes in these denominations had been introduced during World War I, but prior to 1928 they had been issued by the Treasury.) The 'fiver' (see image on page 30) remained simple, white and printed on one side only until a blue version was introduced in 1957.

In 1945, paper money in denominations above £5 ceased to be legal tender, but the pressures of inflation caused the following notes to be issued: £20 in 1970; £10 in 1975; £50 in 1981.

DECIMALISATION

The possibility of converting British currency to a decimal system was first discussed in parliament at the beginning of the nineteenth century, but the earliest practical step in this direction was the introduction of the 'new' florin in 1849. The coin, worth two shillings, was inscribed with the words 'one tenth of a pound'. But the British public proved remarkably resistant to the notion of tampering with its ancient 'base 12' system. It took the government well over a century to commit to decimalisation. Finally, on 1 March 1966 the Chancellor of the Exchequer, Jim Callaghan, announced a heretical plan to chop the pound into 100 equal pieces. Despite impassioned objections, the Decimal Currency Act was passed the following year. D-Day (the 'D' stood for 'decimal') was set for 15 February 1971.

The question now was how to accustom the British to the tricky task of counting in tens. It was decided to break them in gently with a couple of coins that made sense in both systems. The new 5p and 10p pieces, which were introduced in April 1968, were exact equivalents in size and value to the shilling and florin respectively. If both kinds of coin were allowed to coexist for a number of years, hopefully the (new) penny would drop.

The next new coin was the seven-sided 50p introduced in October 1969. The coin was not too much of a threat to traditionalists as they could reassure themselves that it was just a glorified 'ten bob' note. They had no such luxury, however, with the next three decimal coins to be issued. The 2p, 1p and ½p 'coppers' that went into circulation on D-Day were worth 4.8, 2.4 and 1.2 old pennies respectively. It was no use reaching for a pocket calculator as the device had only just been invented and was fiendishly expensive.

The subsequent changes to British coinage have been as follows:

1971 .... 10s note withdrawn and replaced by 50p coin, which had already been in circulation for two years
1980 .... sixpence withdrawn. It had remained in circulation since decimalisation with a value of 2½p
1982 .... 20p and £1 coins introduced. In the same year, the 'new' (as in 'new pence') was dropped from the coinage
1984 .... ½p coin withdrawn
1998 .... bi-metallic £2 coin introduced

MONEY SLANG

 The English love to use nicknames for their coins and banknotes. An understanding of some of the older, pre-decimal, slang terms is very handy when you're watching old films or dealing with cockney pensioners.

Joey – A threepenny bit. Confusingly, it originally referred to a fourpenny bit, or groat, but the usage changed when the groat was discontinued.

Daddler – Another term for a threepenny bit, emphasising the coin's small size.

Tanner – A sixpence (6d). The word probably derives from the Romany Gypsy *tawno*, meaning 'a little one'.

Bob – A shilling. Came into use in the late eighteenth century. One intriguing explanation for the term connects it to bell ringing, in which a 'bob' is a change of the order in which the bells are rung. As the word 'shilling' is derived from the German *skell*, meaning to sound or ring, there may be something in this. An alternative theory is that 'bob' is a shortened form of 'bawbee', an old word for a half penny.

Quid – A pound. *Quid* is the Latin word for 'that' or 'what', as in the expression *quid pro quo* (something for something else). Thought to have come into popular usage in the late seventeenth century.

Nicker – Another word for a pound, possibly referring to the use of nickel in the minting of coins.

Lady Godiva – Rhyming slang for a fiver (£5), commemorating the medieval baroness who rode naked through the streets of Coventry.

Score – £20. 'Score' is an old term for 20, as in the biblical phrase 'threescore years and ten'. The word apparently derives from an ancient method of counting sheep, whereby shepherds would 'score' or cut a notch in a stick every time they got to 20.

Pony – £25. Usage dates from the late 1700s. One theory is that the term derives from a small horse once depicted on an Indian 25 rupee note.

Ton – £100. Derives from the use of the word 'ton' to describe a volume of 100 cubic feet.

Monkey – £500. As with the 'pony', the nickname probably originally referred to an animal depicted on an Indian banknote, in this case worth 500 rupees.

THE GUINEA

On 6 February 1663, a new coin was minted from gold mined in Guinea, west Africa. It was initially worth a pound or 20 shillings, but for self-explanatory reasons everyone referred to it as a guinea. The 'heads' side of the earliest guineas featured the profile of King Charles II on its own, but on subsequent versions the elephant or elephant and castle symbol of the Royal African Company was stamped underneath.

During the first 54 years of its existence the value of the guinea fluctuated with the price of gold (usually upwards), but in 1717 it was fixed at 21 shillings. The pound replaced the guinea in 1816, but the old denomination continued to be used for accounting purposes and by those who considered themselves upper class. During the nineteenth century, tradesmen tended to be paid in pounds and gentlemen in guineas. The guinea is still used in some contexts, notably livestock auctions and horse racing. The first two of the five 'classics' of the English flat season are still known as the Thousand and Two Thousand Guineas (they are for fillies and colts respectively), although the prizes on offer are now considerably more valuable.

MAUNDY MONEY

Every year on the day before Good Friday, the Queen hands out gifts to one elderly man or woman for every year of her age. The recipients, who are chosen for Christian service to their communities, are given two old-fashioned leather string purses. The first, which is red, is filled with ordinary coinage. The second, white, purse contains specially minted 'Maundy' coins, with a total value in pence again equivalent to the monarch's age. In 2007, for example, the Queen was 81, so each of the selected pensioners received 81p in Maundy money. They also received, in the red purse, a £5 coin issued to mark her diamond wedding anniversary.

The word 'Maundy' is derived from the Latin *mandatum*, meaning 'commandment'. The *mandatum* that the ceremony commemorates is Jesus's post-Last Supper instruction to his disciples to 'love one another', issued (according to John, chapter 13) after he had washed their feet. From as early as the fourth century, bishops have been in the habit of echoing Jesus's actions by washing the feet of members of their congregations on Maundy Thursday. This gesture of humility has traditionally been accompanied by gifts of food and clothing.

At some point in the Middle Ages, the English royal family decided to get in on the act. The first monarch recorded as having taken part in the ceremony was Edward II (1307-1327). His successor Edward III was involved to the extent of washing a few feet himself, an example followed by every ruler up to and including James II (1685-1688). When William III (1688-1702)

elected to have a courtier perform the task in his stead, the diarist Samuel
Pepys was deeply shocked. Looked at in this historical light, the Maundy
gifts of today can be seen as substitutes, the contents of the red purse taking
the place of the traditional food and clothing, and the Maundy money for
the foot washing.

Prior to the reign of Charles II (1660-1685), the annual royal handout took the form of ordinary silver coins. Special Maundy money was first minted in 1662. Then, as now, the coins came in four denominations: a groat (four pence), a 'thre'penny bit', a half groat (two pence) and a penny. Today's Maundy coins are minted in 92.5% silver and, unlike regular currency, feature the 'original' 1953 portrait of the Queen. Although they are legal tender, it would be slightly crazy for the recipients to use them as cash as they are eminently collectable.

BRITANNIA

From AD43 to 410, the part of Great Britain corresponding to England and Wales was a province of the Roman Empire known to its conquerors as 'Britannia'. The word was derived from *pretani*, the name that the Greek explorer Pythias of Massalia had found the inhabitants of Cornwall using to refer to themselves when he visited the region in the fourth century BC.

The Romans were great ones for personifying regions and abstract qualities as human females, and this is exactly what they did with Britannia. In about AD119, the Emperor Hadrian struck a copper coin that depicted Britannia as a sullen but warlike figure crouched on a rock holding a shield and spear. The coin was probably minted to commemorate the victories that led to the construction of Hadrian's Wall, a barrier erected across the northern border of the province to keep the Scots at bay.

Britannia on a bronze *sestertius* from
the reign of Antonius Pius (AD138-161)

'Britannia coins' were minted by several of Hadrian's successors, but after
the Romans abandoned Britain in 410 her image fell into obscurity. It was not
revived until 1672, when she was placed on the back of a new issue of copper
farthings and half pennies. They were loosely modelled on the Hadrian coin,
but Britannia's posture was altogether more confident. Instead of resting her
chin on her right hand she was now using it to hold a sprig of olive, and her
shield was decorated with the Union Jack. Samuel Pepys was convinced that
the model for this Britannia was Frances Stewart, Duchess of Richmond and
a mistress of King Charles II.

Having made her debut on coins, Britannia became a fixture on Bank of
England banknotes. On 30 July 1694, three days after the Bank received its

royal charter, the directors voted the common seal should depict 'Britannia sitting on looking on a Bank of Mony' [sic]. She has consistently appeared on the nation's notes and coins ever since. She has, however, changed position from time to time. During the reign of George IV (1820-1830), Britannia's coin persona developed a helmet, dropped the olive branch and turned to face the right. This image, with slight variations, remained on half pennies and farthings until 1937 and on pennies until 1967. Exceptionally, she stood up for the florins issued under Edward VII (1901-1910) but she soon sat down again. When the 50p coin was unveiled in 1969, she was still brandishing the trident that had replaced the original spear since the late eighteenth century, but had also retrieved her olive branch.

The image of Britannia used on banknotes has also changed on several occasions. Two of the most memorable versions have been modelled on the artists' daughters. From 1855 to 1961, the portrait of Britannia used on English notes was actually Daniel Maclise RA's 18-year-old daughter, dressed in Saxon clothing and looking straight at the viewer. She popped up again in the hologram on the Series E £20 note introduced in 1990. Reynolds Stone, who was commissioned to design a new £5 note in 1963, also based his Britannia on an 18-year-old, in this case his daughter, Phillida. She is now a successful children's book illustrator.

Britannia is still there on the front of contemporary English banknotes. She sits in a foil hologram along with the denomination figure, or, in the case of the Series F £20 note, inside a small medallion at bottom left.

WHO'S WHO ON ENGLISH BANKNOTES?

The practice of depicting figures other than the monarch on English banknotes was introduced in 1970 when the Bank of England released its 'Series D' of banknotes. Here is a complete list of the historical characters whose portraits have appeared on Bank of England notes, together with the relevant denominations, plus a few words about the subjects:

SERIES D

£1 – Isaac Newton (issued 9 February 1978, withdrawn 11 March 1988)
Mathematician and physicist who discovered gravity. Seemingly incongruously, he was also Master of the Royal Mint. (Lived 1642 to 1727.)

£5 – Duke of Wellington (issued 11 November 1971, withdrawn 29 November 1991)
Arthur Wellesley, 1st Duke of Wellington, defeated Napoleon at the Battle of Waterloo in 1815. Went on to serve as British Prime Minister twice. (Lived 1769 to 1852.)

£10 – Florence Nightingale (issued 20 February 1975, withdrawn 20 May 1994)
Hospital reformer famous for her nursing work during the Crimean War (1853 to 1856). Ironically, the 'Lady of the Lamp' was a terrible hypochondriac. (Lived 1820 to 1910.)

£20 – William Shakespeare (issued 9 July 1970, withdrawn 19 March 1993)
English poet and playwright now regarded as Britain's and arguably the world's

greatest-ever playwright. His 37 plays include *Hamlet*, *Romeo and Juliet* and *Macbeth*. (Lived 1564 to 1616.)

£50 – Christopher Wren (issued 20 March 1981, withdrawn 20 September 1996)
Architect, mathematician and astronomer. Considered his greatest achievement the construction of St Paul's Cathedral in London. (Lived 1632 to 1723.)

SERIES E
£5 – George Stephenson (issued 7 June 1990, withdrawn 21 November 2003)
Engineer and builder of the world's first steam locomotive. (Lived 1781 to 1848.)

£10 – Charles Dickens (issued 29 April 1992, withdrawn 31 July 2003)
Britain's most famous novelist. Author of *Great Expectations*, *David Copperfield* and *Oliver Twist*. (Lived 1812 to 1870.)

£20 – Michael Faraday (issued 5 June 1991, withdrawn 28 February 2001)
Physicist and chemist. Discovered electromagnetic induction, the key to making electricity a practical tool rather than a curiosity. (Lived 1791 to 1867.)

£50 – John Houblon (issued 20 April 1994, still in circulation)
Probably the least famous person to feature on a British banknote, he was the first governor of the Bank of England. The Bank, which is known as 'The old lady

of Threadneedle Street', is located on the site of his former house in the City of London. (Lived 1632 to 1712.)

SERIES E REVISION

£5 – Elizabeth Fry (issued 21 May 2002, still in circulation)
Prison reformer, best known for her work in Newgate Prison. Was married to a nephew of the founder of the JS Fry chocolate company and had to give up her philanthropic work when he went bankrupt. (Lived 1780 to 1845.)

£10 – Charles Darwin (issued 7 November 2000, still in circulation)
Author of *On the Origin of Species*, in which he propounded the theory of evolution. Grandson of the potter Josiah Wedgewood. (Lived 1809 to 1882.)

£20 – Edward Elgar (issued 22 June 1999, still in circulation)
Worcester-based composer. Wrote the *'Enigma' Variations* and *Pomp and Circumstance March No 1*, the orchestral basis for *Land of Hope and Glory*. (Lived 1857 to 1934.)

SERIES F

£20 – Adam Smith (issued 13 March 2007, still in circulation)
Author of *The Wealth of Nations* and a father of modern economics. Using the example of the manufacture of pins, he showed how specialisation could boost economic output. Smith's inclusion on the note was controversial because he was Scottish. Many remarked that the Scots have perfectly good banknotes of their own. (Lived 1723 to 1790.)

THE QUEEN'S HEAD

Although the heads of rulers have appeared on coins for centuries, the first English* banknotes to follow suit were the 10s and £1 notes issued by the Treasury between 1915 and 1928. (The king at the time was George V.) The monarch's head then disappeared from banknotes until 1960, when Queen Elizabeth II agreed to let her image be used for this purpose. As Her Majesty has aged, updated versions of her portrait have been introduced from time to time.

It was possible to play an amusing trick with the old E Series £10 note (1993-2002). If you folded the note in such a way that the upper part of Charles Dickens's face on the reverse was aligned with the upper part of the Queen's on the front, the result was an uncanny image of tennis 'superbrat' John McEnroe.

(The author once went to a wedding attended by the former Prime Minister Margaret Thatcher. None of his friends had the courage to speak to the Iron Lady, so someone suggested a reward of £10 for the first person to do so. One plucky young man decided to break the ice by showing Mrs T the tenner/John McEnroe trick. 'How very interesting,' said Lady Thatcher, spinning on her heels to talk to somebody else.)

---

* Scottish banknotes are another story. Notes bearing the portraits of Georges II, III and IV were printed by the Royal Bank of Scotland during the eighteenth and early nineteenth centuries.

THE US DOLLAR

ORIGIN OF THE NAME

Strange as it may seem, the word 'dollar' is derived from the name of a town in the Czech Republic. First minted in 1519, the *thaler* (pronounced with a hard 't') was a coin made from silver mined in Joachimsthal, a town in what was then known as Bohemia. *Thal* or *tal* is German for 'valley', so the literal meaning of 'dollar' is 'from the valley'. Europe had been crying out for a new precious metal coin as it had been haemorrhaging gold and silver to the Far East and south-east Asia to pay for silks, spices and other exotica. The *thaler* fitted the bill perfectly. It became a standard European coin and held that position for four centuries.

Interestingly, the word 'dollar' (the Anglicised version of *thaler*) appeared in the works of William Shakespeare some 180 years before it became the name of the official currency of the United States:

That now Sweno, the Norway's King, craves composition;
Nor would we deign him burial of his men
Till he disbursed at Saint Colme's Inch
Ten thousand dollars to our general use.

– *Macbeth* Act I, Scene 2

As time went on, the term 'dollar' began to be applied to coins similar to the *thaler* irrespective of their place of origin. A prime example was the Spanish eight-real coin, or the 'piece of eight' as it is more familiarly known to fans of pirate stories. As a result of a shortage of British currency, this coin was legal tender in pre-revolutionary America, as was the so-called Marie Therese *thaler* from the Austro-Hungarian Empire. It was therefore only natural for the Congress of the United States to choose the name 'dollar' for the currency of the newly formed nation in 1785.

THE HISTORY OF AMERICAN MONEY

WAMPUM

The ancestor of North American currency was wampum. It consisted of polished shell beads that the continent's native tribes traditionally strung into belts. Strictly speaking, wampum refers only to white beads, which were usually made from the shells of the North Atlantic Channelled Whelk (*Busycotypus canaliculatus*) or the Knobbled Whelk (*Busycotypus carica*). Black or purple beads known as *suckanhock* were also used. They were made from the Quahog Clam (*Mercenaria mercenaria*) and were slightly more valuable. However, nobody will mind if we generically refer to both kinds of bead as wampum.

It is a mistake to describe wampum in its original form as money. What can be said with confidence is the indigenous Americans regarded it as extremely important. The patterns into which the beads of wampum belts were woven stored and conveyed vital information. They were used to call meetings, mark treaties, order ceremonies, cement marriages and much more besides.

Although wampum was not money as such, it quickly took on that function after the arrival of European settlers. It was, after all, valued, scarce, durable and easily divisible. The new arrivals found they could use it to purchase all sorts of things from the native tribes, including land and labour. In 1664, Peter Stuyvesant borrowed wampum worth more than 5,000 guilders to pay the wages of workers building the New York citadel. By the following century, the Europeans were using steel drills to manufacture wampum in enormous quantities. This led to serious devaluation. Nevertheless, production continued well into the nineteenth century.

JW Campbell's wampum factory in New Jersey, which was founded in 1760, remained in business for 100 years.

PRE-REVOLUTIONARY CURRENCY

The Pilgrim Fathers and their successors found themselves in a tricky position as far as money was concerned. Because they lived in a British colony, the official currency was the pound. Unfortunately, it was illegal to export cash from the mother country. There was therefore an acute shortage of coins. (Paper money had yet to enter the picture.) Nevertheless, the settlers were an ingenious bunch who found various ways to get around the problem:

Barter – As most people lived on the land, the scarcity of hard currency was less of a problem than it would have been in a more urban and industrialised society. Agricultural products were freely bartered and often used to pay taxes. In South Carolina, for example, the value of a bushel of corn was officially set at two shillings. Jewellery, slaves and gold plate were also used for bartering.

Native currencies – When it came to dealing with the 'Indians', the settlers quickly discovered that wampum and furs were much more useful than coins. In time, they began to use these forms of currency among themselves. In 1637, the authorities of Massachusetts made wampum legal tender up to the value of a shilling.

Commodity money – Gold and silver were always acceptable as forms of payment. In and around Virginia, so was tobacco, either raw or in the form of 'transfer notes'. These were certificates attesting to the value, in English currency, of tobacco deposited at central warehouses. In 1727, the government of Virginia made tobacco notes legal tender.

Foreign coins – Without a sufficient supply of British coinage, the Colonists turned to foreign alternatives. Spanish and Portuguese coins were particularly popular, among them the fabled pieces of eight. The use of foreign coins was not too problematic so long as everyone agreed on what they were worth, but this was not always easy. For one thing, the value of foreign coins could change, just as it does today. For another, many were in the habit of 'clipping' coins, ie cutting away some of their constituent metal in the hope they could still use them, while acquiring a stash of commodity money on the side.

Meanwhile, several colonies muddied the waters in the early eighteenth century by raising the value of foreign coins in the hope of getting their neighbours to spend them in their territories.

Privately minted coins – In 1652, John Hall of Massachusetts began minting his own 'pine tree shillings'. The coins, which took their name from the image with which they were stamped, proved very popular, but the British forced Hall to close down his mint in 1684.

Bills of exchange – The bill of exchange was an important mechanism for obtaining supplies from Europe. As it was illegal to export money from Britain, when an American merchant sent goods to be sold in the UK, the proceeds would be held on his behalf by a Commission Merchant in London. The former could then instruct the latter to use some of his credit to purchase goods and ship them back across the Atlantic. American businessmen who did not have credit in Britain could buy it (for a fee) from those who did.

EARLY NOTES

The first paper money in what would become the United States was issued by the Massachusetts Bay Colony in 1690 to finance an ill-fated military expedition to Quebec. Other colonies soon followed suit, printing money in anticipation of tax revenues and using it to purchase supplies and pay troops. The system worked reasonably well until certain colonies got greedy. A notable offender was Rhode Island, which printed far more money than it could ever hope to recoup through taxation. This led to runaway inflation. As the colonies were in the habit of accepting each others' currency, the effects rapidly spread to Rhode Island's neighbours.

The eighteenth century also saw the rise of 'land banks'. These were institutions that printed their own money and lent it on the basis of property mortgages.

The emergence of these two types of banknote only served to confuse an already complicated situation. In 1775, the North Carolina authorities listed no less than 17 forms of money as legal tender. The failure of the British to provide the American colonies with an adequate monetary system was a major impetus behind the War of Independence.

CONTINENTAL CURRENCY

To finance the Revolution against Britain, the Continental Congress (the forerunner of the independent US government) authorised the issue of America's first national currency in 1775. 'Continentals', as the banknotes were known, did the job for which they were created, but they quickly depreciated as they were not backed by gold, silver or anything else. By the end of the war, they were worth about a thousandth of their nominal value, hence the damning phrase 'not worth a continental'.

ADOPTION OF THE DOLLAR

In 1785, the Continental Congress declared that the dollar rather than the pound would be the currency of the new independent nation and would replace the various state currencies. The first coins were struck at the US Mint in Philadelphia eight years later. Congress also moved to centralise banking operations. In 1791, it granted a 20-year charter to America's first central bank. The appropriately named First Bank of the United States was authorised to print national banknotes and empowered to regulate the activities of commercial banks throughout the land. Although the bank was a financial success, its charter was allowed to lapse in 1811. The commercial banks' response to its demise was to print far too many banknotes, leading to five years of inflationary chaos. In 1816, the Second Bank of the United States was established, again with a 20-year charter. Unfortunately, it was not popular with those who sought easy credit and pressure began to mount to do away with it.

FREE BANKING ERA AND BROKEN NOTES

In 1832, President Andrew Jackson revoked the Second Bank of the United States' charter. This ushered in an era during which banking was subject to minimal regulation. Local, state-chartered banks began to spring up everywhere. By 1836 there were some 1,600 of them. With a bewildering array of more than 30,000 different notes in circulation, forgery became easy and therefore rife. To make matters worse, some of the banks were a lot less than scrupulous. In the absence of strict controls regarding the backing of

UNITED STATES OF AMERICA

E
PLURIBUS
UNUM

ONE DOLLAR

MINTED 51

banknotes with precious metals, many banks operated with scarcely any reserves behind them. They went bust with such frequency that their issues became known as 'broken notes'. Then there were the 'wildcat' banks. These institutions printed notes that stated they could be redeemed for gold or silver and then located themselves in such out-of-the-way places there was little danger of this actually happening. It was said they were more accessible to wildcats than to human beings, hence the name.

THE CIVIL WAR AND THE NATIONALISATION OF AMERICAN CURRENCY

The Civil War (1861-1865) began when South Carolina, fearing that the newly elected president, Abraham Lincoln, intended to abolish slavery, seceded from the Union. It was soon joined by six other states (Alabama, Florida, Georgia, Louisiana, Mississippi and Texas) and four months later by four more (Arkansas, North Carolina, Tennessee and Virginia). In February 1861, the seceding states formed an independent government known as the Confederacy. The United States was now split in two.

The Confederate constitution guaranteed the rights of member states to issue their own banknotes. To fund the war effort, they did this in a big way, as did the central Confederacy government. The sheer volume of banknotes produced caused massive inflation, as did a flood of forged notes introduced into the Confederacy by the opposing Union side in a bid to further harm the Southern economy.

The Union took a very different approach to war finance. In 1861, Congress introduced 'Demand Notes' in $5, $10 and $20 denominations. Because the reverse sides of these were printed in green ink, they became known as 'greenbacks'. The notes stated they were redeemable in coin and they still are.

In 1862, Demand Notes were replaced by Legal Tender Notes, also known as United States Notes. For the first time, the US had a currency that was by law good for all debts, both public and private. United States Notes were initially backed by nothing more than faith in the government, but in 1877 they became redeemable in silver. The last United States Notes were issued in 1966.

FRACTIONAL CURRENCY

One of the side effects of the Civil War was that people began to hoard coins. This led to a serious shortage, which was exacerbated by the fact that all available metal was needed for manufacturing weapons. To replace the 'missing' coins, in 1863 the Union government issued what was known as 'fractional currency'. This took the form of small notes in three, five, 10, 15, 25 and 50 cent denominations. They were last issued in 1876.

NATIONAL BANK NOTES

In 1863, Congress passed the National Banking Act, which effectively tied the banking system to a uniform currency. State banks were not actually banned, but the imposition of a 10% tax on the notes they issued quickly killed them off. To complement the Act, yet another form of currency was introduced: the National Bank Note. From 1863 to 1877, National Bank Notes were printed by private firms operating under strict governmental guidelines. At the end of this period, the newly formed US Bureau of Engraving and Printing took over the printing of all government notes, a role it still holds. Nevertheless, National Bank Notes continued to be issued by private banks until 1935 using pre-printed paper provided by the Bureau.

THE FEDERAL RESERVE BANK

You probably have a headache by now and so will be pleased to learn that we are reaching the end of a long story. The final brick in the construction of the current American monetary system was the establishment of the Federal Reserve Bank in 1913. This institution was founded by President Woodrow Wilson to 'supplant the dictatorship of the private banking institutions' and 'stabilise the inflexibility of… bank note supplies'. The first Federal Reserve banknotes were introduced in 1914. They are now the only form of paper money issued in the US.

The Federal Reserve Bank pays the Bureau of Engraving and Printing approximately four cents for every note. It then distributes them to commercial banks, so long as they pay for them by drawing down money from the reserves. The Federal Reserve Bank is also responsible for the distribution of coins, which it buys from the US Mint (a division of the Treasury) at face value.

THE DOLLAR SIGN

There are several theories about the origin of the US dollar sign ($). A key question is which version you consider more authentic, the one with one vertical line or its rival with two. The three most popular explanations are:

1. The sign is derived from the initials for 'United States'. If a 'U' is superimposed over an 'S' and the lower part of the 'U' is left out, you end up with an 'S' plus two parallel lines.

2. The sign is an evolved form of the symbol for Spanish pesos. This consisted of a 'P' with a small 's' next to it. If you simplify the 'P' to a vertical line, blow up the 's' and combine the two images, you get an 'S' with a single stroke through it. This may seem a little convoluted, but the strength of the argument is that the eight peso coin was widely used in America prior to the Revolution.

3. The sign rightly has two parallel lines and is descended from the Spanish coat of arms illustrated right. This consists of two pillars (the 'Pillars of Hercules') with a ribbon bearing the motto *Plus ultra* winding between them. If you turn this image on its side, you end up with something not totally unlike the dollar symbol.

THE PYRAMID AND THE EYE

Nothing rouses paranoia like the pyramid/eye motif on the back of the $1 bill. The design, which is officially known as 'the Great Seal of the United States', was chosen by Congress as a means of endorsing government documents on 20 June 1782.

The front of the seal (and the dollar bill) is relatively uncontroversial. It depicts a bald eagle (the national bird) holding 13 arrows, representing the 13 original States of the Union, in its left talon, and an olive branch, symbolising a desire for peace, in its right. Clutched in its beak is the motto *E Pluribus Unum* ('Out of many, one'), which refers both to the collective strength of the United States and the diverse ethnic origins of its inhabitants.

The reverse of the seal/dollar bill is another matter. Its central motif is an unfinished pyramid with an eye floating at its apex and radiating light. Above the eye is the motto *Annuit Coeptis*, which means 'It [the eye] has' approved our beginnings', and below the pyramid are the words *Novus Ordo Seclorum* ('A new order for the ages'), which are lifted straight from Virgil. The conventional interpretation is that the unfinished pyramid represents the state of the nation when the image was designed – it had a powerful base but was very much a work in progress – and the all-seeing eye stands for God. But try telling that to a conspiracy theorist. To such folk, the reverse of the Great Seal is proof the nation (and possibly the world) is run by a sinister cabal of Freemasons.

It is true that one and perhaps two of the original design committee were Masons (Benjamin Franklin certainly was and Thomas Jefferson may well have been) and it is true that Freemasons are keen on pyramids and frequently use the 'Eye of Providence' motif. But it is also true that there is no record of them combining the images, unless you argue in a circular fashion from the evidence of the seal itself. Furthermore, the all-seeing eye was a well-known renaissance symbol (there is one on Aachen Cathedral) and Egyptian civilisation was much admired during the eighteenth century. In the end, the choice is yours. Is the back of the dollar bill a coded message to insiders or merely a reflection of popular iconography in an era when the Great Seal was designed?

PEOPLE AND PLACES DEPICTED ON US BANKNOTES

Under Title 31, Section 5114(b) of the United States Code, only images of the deceased may appear on US currency.

For the purpose of (relative) brevity, we've decided to stick to individuals whose portraits have featured fairly prominently on US banknotes. If we were to list all of the signatories to the Declaration of Independence who appear on the back of the $2 bill, for instance, we'd be here all day.

CURRENT BANKNOTES

The individuals whose portraits appear on the fronts of the US banknotes have remained the same since 1929, the year in which the dimensions of the notes were reduced to their current levels.

$1..............................Face – George Washington (1732-1799, 1st US President)
Reverse – Pyramid/eye motif ('the Great Seal')

$2..............................Face – Thomas Jefferson (1743-1826, 3rd US President)
Reverse – Signing of the Declaration of Independence

$5.............................Face – Abraham Lincoln (1809-1865, 16th US President)
Reverse – Lincoln Memorial

$10...........................Face – Alexander Hamilton (1755-1804,
1st Secretary of the Treasury)
Reverse – US Treasury Building

$20 ....Face – Andrew Jackson (1767-1845, 7th US President)
Reverse – The White House

$50 ....Face – Ulysses Grant (1822-1885, 18th US President)
Reverse – US Capitol

$100 ....Face – Benjamin Franklin (1706-1790, statesman,
inventor of the lightning rod)
Reverse – Independence Hall

⇒

HIGH DENOMINATION NOTES WITHDRAWN IN 1969

These notes are no longer in circulation, but are worth knowing about for quiz purposes:

$500 .... Face – William McKinley (1843-1901, 25th US President)
Reverse – Numeral 500 and the ornamental phrase
'Five Hundred Dollars'

$1,000 .... Face – Grover Cleveland (1837-1908, 22nd & 24th US President)
Reverse – Numeral 1,000 and the ornamental phrase
'One Thousand Dollars'

$5,000 .... Face – James Madison (1751-1836, 4th US President)
Reverse – Numeral 5,000 and the ornamental phrase
'Five Thousand Dollars'

$10,000 .... Face – Salmon Chase (1808-1873, US Secretary of the Treasury
under Lincoln)
Reverse – Numeral 10,000 and the ornamental phrase
'Ten Thousand Dollars'

$100,000* .... Face – Woodrow Wilson (1856-1924, 28th US President)
Reverse – Numeral 100,000 and the ornamental phrase
'One Hundred Thousand Dollars'

* The $100,000 note never appeared in general circulation. It was used in transactions between Federal Reserve Banks.

HISTORICAL FIGURES ON THE REVERSE OF WITHDRAWN BANKNOTES

$10,000 (Reverse), circulated 1918-1928 – John Carver (1576-1621), first governor of Plymouth Colony

$10,000 (Reverse), circulated 1918-1928 – William Bradford (1590-1657), second governor of Plymouth Colony

$10,000 (Reverse), circulated 1918-1928 – William Brewster (1566-1644), pastor of Plymouth Colony

$10,000 (Reverse), circulated 1918-1928 – John Robinson (1575-1625), organiser of the *Mayflower* voyage

$10,000 (Reverse), circulated 1918-1928 – Myles Standish (1584-1656), military commander of Plymouth Colony

$5,000 (Reverse), circulated 1918-1928 – Elbridge Gerry (1744-1814), delegate at the Continental Congress 1782 to 1785

$5,000 (Reverse), circulated 1918-1928 – Thomas Jefferson (1743-1826), delegate at the Continental Congress 1783 to 1784

$5,000 (Reverse), circulated 1918-1928 – James Madison (1751-1836), delegate at the Continental Congress 1780 to 1783

$5,000 (Reverse), circulated 1918-1928 – Thomas Mifflin (1744-1800), president of the United States in Congress Assembled 1783 to 1784

$5,000 (Reverse), circulated 1918-1928 – James Monroe (1758-1831), delegate at the Continental Congress 1783 to 1786

$5,000 (Reverse), circulated 1918-1928 – George Washington (1732-1799), commander-in-chief of Continental Army 1775 to 1783

$500 (Reverse), circulated 1918-1928 – Hernando de Soto (1496-1542), Spanish discoverer of the Mississippi River

$500 (Reverse), circulated 1929-1969 – William McKinley (1843-1901), 25th US President

AVERAGE LIFESPAN OF AMERICAN NOTES

$1	21 months
$5	16 months
$10	18 months
$20	24 months
$50	55 months
$100	89 months

'IN GOD WE TRUST'

In 1957, Congress passed a law that required all the nation's coins and banknotes to bear the motto 'In God We Trust'. Aside from a desire to obtain divine approval, the motive for this move was probably a desire to distinguish the US from the 'godless' Soviet Union. The motto first appeared on the series of banknotes issued in 1963. The law requiring its use has been challenged many times but the courts have stood firm.

'ILLEGAL' BANKNOTES

In November 2006, Federal Judge James Robertson made a ruling that raised eyebrows. He declared the paper currency of the United States illegal. The reason given was one with which millions of visitors to the country can sympathise. All American banknotes are the same size and colour. A $100 bill looks and feels much the same as a one dollar bill. This causes enough difficulties if you merely let your concentration lapse. If you are blind, the consequences can be devastating. Robertson deemed that through its failure to provide visually impaired people with a way of distinguishing between notes of different denominations, the Treasury Department was guilty of unlawful discrimination. He gave the Department 30 days to commence discussions on potential remedies to the problem. Possibilities include marking the bills with raised numerals and perforated dots or printing them in different sizes.

No doubt motivated by a combination of innate conservatism and concern about the cost of revamping the banknote system, the Bush administration announced its intention to appeal the decision. The crux of its argument was that visually impaired people are not denied 'meaningful access' to the value of their notes because they always have the option of investing in portable currency readers. These devices, however, retail for around $300 (£150).

The case promises to rumble on. In the meantime, readers worried about possessing these legally dubious pieces of paper are welcome to send them in to the author.

THE EURO

In December 2006, the euro surpassed the US dollar in terms of the combined value of notes in circulation (€610 billion, equivalent at the time to $802 billion, compared with approximately $770 billion in US currency). It is now the world's most popular form of cash.

THE PARTICIPANTS

The euro is used by more than 315 million people in the European Union on a daily basis. As of summer 2007, it was the official currency of 13 member states of the European Union, plus various principalities and overseas territories. A further 12 EU states were due to adopt the euro at dates specified with varying precision, with two more (the UK and Denmark) intending to opt out for the foreseeable future. The complete list of participants in the so-called single currency is as follows:

EU MEMBER STATES ALREADY USING THE EURO

NATION	DATE OF ADOPTION
Austria	1 January 1999
Belgium	1 January 1999
Finland	1 January 1999
France	1 January 1999
Germany	1 January 1999

500
200
100
BCE ECB EZB EKT EKP
50
BCE ECB EZB EKT EKP 2002
20
BCE ECB EZB EKT EKP 2002
BCE ECB EZB EKT EKP 2002
10
10
10
5

Ireland	1 January 1999
Italy	1 January 1999
Luxembourg	1 January 1999
The Netherlands	1 January 1999
Portugal	1 January 1999
Spain	1 January 1999
Greece	1 January 2001
Slovenia	1 January 2007

MEMBER STATES DUE TO ADOPT THE EURO

NATION	DATE OF ADOPTION
Malta	1 January 2008
Cyprus	1 February 2008
Slovakia	1 January 2009
Bulgaria	1 January 2010
Estonia	1 January 2010
Hungary	1 January 2010
Lithuania	1 January 2010
Poland	Initially set for January 2010, may now be delayed
Czech Republic	Not before 2010
Latvia	Not before 2010
Sweden	Not before 2012
Romania	Not before 2014

NON EU-EUROPEAN STATES THAT HAVE ADOPTED THE EURO

These states are allowed to mint limited numbers of their own euro coins:
Monaco, Vatican City, San Marino

EUROPEAN COUNTRIES AND TERRITORIES WITH EURO AS DE FACTO CURRENCY

Andorra, Kosovo, Montenegro

NON-EUROPEAN TERRITORIES OF EU STATES
WHERE EURO IS USED

TERRITORY	LOCATION	NATIONALITY
Guadeloupe	Caribbean	French overseas department
French Guiana	South America	French overseas department
Martinique	Caribbean	French overseas department
Réunion	Indian Ocean	French overseas department
Saint-Pierre et Miquelon	North Atlantic	French territorialcommunity
Mayotte	Indian Ocean	French territorial community
Territoire des Terres Australes et Antarctiques Françaises	Southern Indian Ocean and Antarctica	Uninhabited French territory visited by tourists
Azores	Atlantic Ocean	Portuguese
Madeira	Atlantic Ocean	Portuguese
Canary Islands	Atlantic Ocean	Spanish
Ceuta	Northern Morocco	Spanish autonomous community
Melilla	Northern Morocco	Spanish autonomous community
Islas Chafarinas*	Off Moroccan coast	Spanish
Peñón de Alhucemas*	Off Moroccan coast	Spanish
Peñón de Vélez de la Gomera*	Off Moroccan coast	Spanish

These Spanish islands would use the euro were it not for the fact that they are uninhabited.

VARADERO

This one comes straight out of left field. Since 1 June 2002, the euro has been an official currency of Varadero, Cuba's most famous beach resort. In an experiment designed to attract European tourists, the town's hotels, shops and restaurants now post prices in euros and accept the currency without converting it into local pesos. If the scheme proves successful, the rest of Cuba may take up the euro.

THE EURO SYMBOL

According the European Commission, the euro symbol is 'inspired by the Greek epsilon, which points back to the cradle of European civilisation, and [by] the first letter of "Europe" crossed by two parallel lines to indicate the stability of the euro'. It is also easy to reproduce on old-fashioned typewriters. All you have to do is type a capital 'C', go back a space and then hit the equals key (=).

The official line is that the symbol was designed by a team led by the Belgian Alain Billiet, but this is hotly disputed by supporters of a German nonagenerian named Arthur Eisenmenger. His version of events is that he drew the symbol in his Luxembourg office just before retiring as chief graphic designer of the then European Economic Community in the mid-1970s. He then sent the design to the European Commission in Brussels, where it languished in a drawer for more than 20 years. When he saw EC President Jacques Santer unveil the euro symbol on television in 1997, his eyes popped out of his head. According to his wife Mechthild, he leapt from his chair shouting 'Look, that's my E, my E!'

Eisenmenger has admitted that he wasn't thinking about currency when he doodled the original '€'. He was merely trying to come up with a design to symbolise Europe. He isn't after money for his creation, just recognition. 'A thank you would be nice,' Mechthild told *The Observer* newspaper in 2001.

The claim is backed up by the French illustrator Julien Bozzola, who was Eisenmenger's colleague at the time of the alleged moment of inspiration. 'He was the E-fanatic in the office, always working on Es for this and that,' Bozzola has said. 'His name begins with the letter, so it was also somehow a personal undertaking for him.'

THE BANKNOTES

How do you design banknotes that feel quintessentially European without offending any of the EU nations? If you were to plonk the Eiffel Tower on the €10 note, for example, the Italians would no doubt scream: 'What about the Colosseum?' If you then put the Colosseum on one of the six remaining euro denominations, you'd still leave the majority of EU members without a representative monument. The answer turned out to be to use images of architectural features generic enough to be unmistakably European but not specific enough to make obvious references to particular countries.

The man who came up with this solution was an employee of the Oesterreichische (Austrian) Nationalbank called Robert Kalina. In December 1996, the Council of the European Monetary Institute announced he had won its competition to find a designer for the euro banknotes. The theme of Kalina's proposal was 'Ages and styles of Europe'. The front of the notes, which were to be identical throughout the EU, were to feature windows and gateways, symbolising openness. Their backs were to be printed with images of bridges, demonstrating European cooperation and communication. The resulting notes were as follows:

DENOMINATION	COLOUR	SIZE (MM)	ARCHITECTURAL STYLE
€5	Grey	120 x 62	Classical
€10	Red	127 x 67	Romanesque
€20	Blue	133 x 72	Gothic
€50	Orange	140 x 77	Renaissance
€100	Green	147 x 82	Baroque and Rococo
€200	Yellow/Brown	153 x 82	Age of iron and glass
€500	Purple	160 x 82	Modern 20th century

THE COINS

To give the member states an opportunity to express their individual identities in monetary form, the decision was taken for each denomination of euro coin to have a 'common' side showing a map of the EU and the value, and a 'national' side featuring an image chosen by the issuing country. Nevertheless, they were to be usable in any euro-using nation regardless of their country of origin.

The competition to design the common sides of euro coins was won by Luc Luycx, an artist from Belgium:

DENOMINATION	COMMON SIDE	REMARKS
1 cent*	Shows place of Europe	Not used in Finland and
2 cent*	on the globe	the Netherlands, where
5 cent*		prices are rounded to the
		nearest 5 cents
10 cent*	Shows the individual	"
20 cent*	EU countries	"
50 cent*		
€1	Shows the EU without	"
€2**	borders	"

The Greeks, uniquely, use the words lepto *and* lepta *(the plural) in place of 'cent' on the lower denomination coins, only rendered in the Greek alphabet.*

*** Some member states have issued commemorative coins of various other denominations. They are legal tender only in the nation that issued them. Some member states have also replaced the national side of the €2 coin with a special design to commemorate a particular event (eg Greece to mark the 2004 Summer Olympics). These coins are legal tender throughout the euro zone.*

MATERIALS

The 1, 2 and 5 cent coins are made from copper-covered steel. The 10, 20 and 50 cent coins are made from 'Nordic gold', an alloy consisting of copper (89%), aluminium (5%), zinc (5%) and tin (1%).

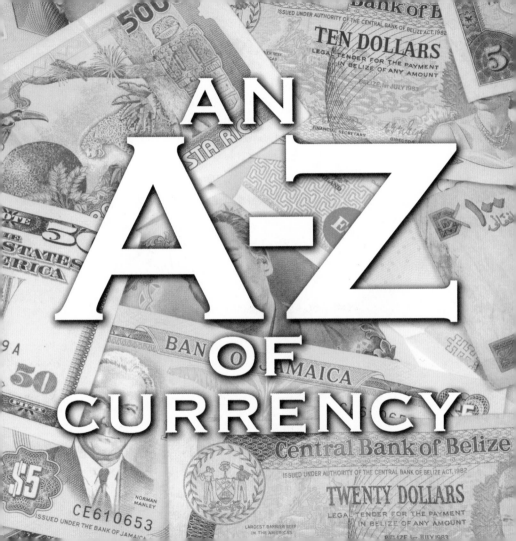

AN
A-Z
OF
CURRENCY

AFGHANISTAN

As a result of the Islamic prohibition on the depiction of living beings, contemporary Afghan banknotes are rather dry affairs, featuring mosques, airport towers and the like. But it was not always this way. Consider this 500 Afghani note from 1991. The front shows some locals playing a spirited game of *buskashi*, a form of polo in which a goat carcass is used instead of a ball:

ANTARCTICA

Argentina, Australia, Chile, France, New Zealand, Norway and the UK have all claimed portions of the frozen landmass at the base of the globe, but the continent has been considered politically neutral since the signing of the Antarctic Treaty in 1959. Aside from the claimant nations, the signatories were Belgium, Japan, South Africa, the US and the USSR.

Given that Antarctica has no government and no permanent population, you might expect it to lack a currency of its own. And to a certain extent, you'd be right. Several nations operate scientific bases and research stations on the continent, but within them most transactions are conducted using the regular currency of the country in question. In 1996, however, an enterprising American/Canadian organisation called the Antarctic Overseas Exchange Office (AOEO) started issuing Antarctic banknotes. The idea was to sell them to tourists and collectors to raise funds for research and humanitarian projects.

The notes are currently available in denominations of 1, 2, 3, 5, 10, 20, 50 and 100 Antarctic dollars, and very pretty they are too. There is just one catch. They are not legal tender in Antarctica or anywhere else. Nevertheless, the AOEO promises to exchange them for their equivalent in US dollars provided they are sent in before their expiry dates. These are printed on the notes and are typically six to nine years after the date of issue. In practice, however, Antarctic dollars are rarely redeemed as they are prized by collectors and sell for significantly more than their face values. It is this that allows the AOEO to cover its costs and raise money for charity. If the Exchange was regularly forced to buy back the notes at the same price they had sold them for, the scheme would rapidly grind to a halt.

ARGENTINA

In 2002, Argentina issued a 2 peso coin to commemorate the 50th anniversary of the death of Eva Peron, everyone's favourite leading lady from an Andrew Lloyd-Webber musical.

BIGGEST BANKNOTE (SIZE)

In 1998, the Philippines printed a limited edition of 1,000 gigantic 100,000 piso banknotes to mark the centenary of the country's independence. With dimensions of 356 x 216mm (14 x 8.5in), the note is the same width as an A4 sheet of paper, but 6cm (2.4in) longer. You need to fold it three or possibly four times to fit it into the average wallet.

The front of this whopper depicts a decisive moment in the history of the Philippines known as the 'Cry of Pugadlawin'. On 23 August 1896, several hundred Filipinos gathered in Pugadlawin in the city of Kalookan and, urged on by their leader Andrés Bonifacio, tore up their *cedulas* (residence certificates) with a shout of 'Long live the Philippines!'. This was the start of an ultimately successful revolt against Spain. Two years later, Filipino independence was declared, an event commemorated on the banknote's reverse.

CHANNEL ISLANDS

The Channel Islands are not technically part of the UK, but they are British Crown Dependencies. The administration of the eight inhabited islands – Jersey, Guernsey, Alderney, Sark, Herm plus the tiny Jethou, Brecqhou and Lihou – is divided between two Bailiwicks: the Bailiwick of Guernsey (all the islands bar Jersey) and the Bailiwick of Jersey. Both issue their own currencies, which are pegged to the UK pound. Either can be used on any of the islands.

JERSEY POUND

The Jersey banknotes all depict Queen Elizabeth II on the front. The denominations, colours and images on the reverses are as follows:

£1 (green)	The Parish Church of St Helier (the capital of Jersey)
£5 (purple)	La Corbière lighthouse
£10 (red)	The death of Major Pierson at the Battle of Jersey (1781)
£20 (blue)	St Ouen's manor
£50 (brown)	Government House

GUERNSEY POUND

Guernsey notes are issued in five denominations: £1 (green), £5 (pink), £10 (blue/orange), £20 (pink) and £50 (brown).

80 MINTED

CONGO

Katanga, or Shaba as it is now known, is a mineral-rich province in the south of the Democratic Republic of Congo. From the tenth century until around the 1920s, the most important form of currency in the region was the handa or Katanga Cross (above, left). This was a cross-shaped ingot made by pouring molten copper into a simple mould cut into sand. Handas were typically about 20cm (8in) across and weighed around 600g (1.3lb). One would buy you 10kg (22lb) of manioc flour, five or six chickens or six axes. Wives were a little dearer at a price of around 14 crosses.

When the Congo obtained independence from Belgium in 1960, Katanga declared itself a separate state. The following year it minted the natty 5 franc coin shown above. It was cast in nine-carat gold and paid tribute to the region's traditional money. But Katangan independence was short-lived. There was no way the Congo's new leader Joseph Mobutu was prepared to countenance the loss of the nation's most lucrative province, and in 1963 Katanga was reabsorbed.

COOK ISLANDS

The Cook Islands has a tiny population (18,700), but the constituent islands are distributed over 2.2 million square kilometres of the South Pacific. It takes around four hours to fly from largest island, Rarotonga, to the northernmost member of the group. The Islands are self-governing, but closely associated with New Zealand. As a result both New Zealand and Cook Island dollars are legal tender in the islands.

In 2006, the Cook Islands issued a remarkable coin to commemorate the 80th anniversary of the invention of television. One side of the copper-nickel $1 coin bears a portrait of Queen Elizabeth II and is conventional enough, but the other side is anything but. It features a picture of John L Baird, the inventor of television, alongside a moving, miniaturised version of his first broadcast. The action consists of a hand moving in front of a puppet.

DISNEY DOLLARS

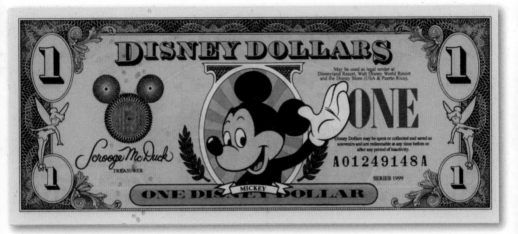

Never an operation to miss a marketing opportunity, the Disney Corporation has been issuing its own currency for more than 20 years. Well, technically it is 'corporate scrip', but you get the point. Disney dollars are sold at various outlets within the company's parallel universe and can be used at most of its stores and theme parks. One Disney dollar is worth US$1 and Disney will freely exchange each currency for the other. The company recognises that a proportion of Disney dollars will never be redeemed because people tend to keep them as souvenirs or, having purchased them, forget that redemption is an option.

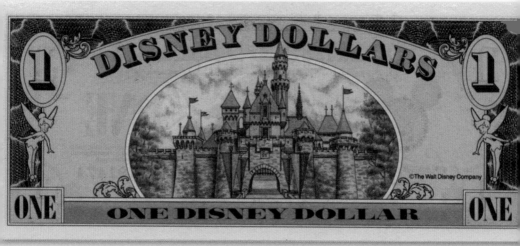

The first Disney dollar notes were a $1 and a $5 issued in May 1987 that featured Mickey Mouse and Goofy respectively. They were followed in November 1989 by a $10 bill adorned with an image of Mickey's partner Minnie. New bills are produced in most years. The characters depicted frequently change and their portraits are usually flanked by a pair of fluttering Tinkerbells. Most of the notes bear the signature of the treasurer, who is naturally Scrooge McDuck, Donald's squillionaire Scottish cousin.

84 MINTED

EQUATORIAL AFRICAN STATES

The Equatorial African States was a monetary union formed in 1961 by a group of former French colonies made up of Cameroon, Chad, Congo (now Congo-Brazzaville), Gabon and Equatorial Guinea. We have included this 5,000-franc banknote (1963) because it features a rather attractive pastoral scene. This particular example comes from Chad.

FALKLAND ISLANDS

The Falkland Islands, or the Islas Malvinas as they like to think of them in Argentina, are a self-governing overseas territory of the UK. The currency, which is called the Falkland pound, retains parity with sterling. Perhaps because the population is only around 3,000, the Islands' fauna features prominently on the local money.

The Queen's head on the banknotes is flanked by seals and penguins and the coins are decorated with an array of creatures. The most interesting is the beast on the back of the 50p coin. Called a *warrah*, it is an indigenous fox last seen in about 1875.

GERMANY

Economists have not agreed on a precise definition of hyperinflation, but for our purposes it is enough to define it as inflation gone mad. Germany is not the only country to have experienced the phenomenon, nor was its version in 1923 the most extreme – that honour goes to Hungary in 1945-1946 (see Highest Denomination on page 96), followed by Yugoslavia in 1993-1994 – but it is the most famous example.

The root cause of German hyperinflation was World War I. The government had accumulated massive debts to finance its war effort and Germany had been ordered to pay huge sums in reparation to the victorious nations at the

Hyperinflation
German woman feeding her stove with banknotes to save money(!)

Treaty of Versailles. The burden was compounded by a fall in production as the economy shifted orientation from war to peace. Before long, Germany's interest payments exceeded its gross domestic product (GDP).

The government's answer to the crisis was to print more money. The trouble was that there was nothing to back it. The country's gold reserves had dwindled to almost zero as a result of reparation payments and economic output was falling rather than rising. The inevitable consequence was inflation. Then the situation worsened considerably. When Germany failed to meet its reparation costs at the end of 1922, the Allies responded by sending Belgian and French troops to occupy the Ruhr, the nation's industrial heartland. Millions of workers went on strike in protest and Germany was deprived of its main source of income.

The printing of new money now went into overdrive and inflation skyrocketed. On 1 January 1923, it took an already frightening 9,000 marks to purchase

$1. By June, the figure had risen to 100,000. Two months later, it stood at 4.62 million and by November $1 was worth an astonishing 4.2 trillion marks. At the peak of hyperinflation, an egg cost 80 billion Marks. Workers had to be paid every morning, as yesterday's wage would now be virtually worthless. Having been handed wheelbarrow-loads of cash, employees would head straight for the shops to spend it before its value had crumbled. And housewives (like the lady in the picture) worked out that it was cheaper to use bundles of cash to light their stoves than to purchase wood.

The madness finally came to an end thanks to Gustav Stresemann, who took over as chancellor in August 1923. He began by ordering the striking Ruhr workers to return to work to kickstart industrial production. Then, on 15 November, he replaced the terminally ailing mark with the Rentenmark at an exchange rate of one trillion to one. As Germany's gold reserves had run dry, the new currency was backed by industrial and agricultural property. Stresemann then halted the printing of new notes and started soliciting foreign investment. As a result, prices began to stabilise. Within a few months, the cost of a loaf of bread had fallen from 500 billion marks to half a Rentenmark.

Amazingly, by 1924 Germany was entering a brief but sweet golden age. The psychological damage, however, was irreversible. Germans who had lost their life savings were on the lookout for scapegoats. They found them in the nations that had imposed the burdens of the Treaty of Versailles, in financiers, many of whom had done very well out of the crisis, and most ominously, in the Jews.

GIBRALTAR

Gibraltar is home to Europe's only monkey, the Barbary macaque, or the Barbary ape as is it is often called. According to popular legend, if the apes were to leave Gibraltar, the British would lose control of the rocky island at the western end of the Mediterranean.

There is a thriving population of some 200 of the tailless simians on the Upper Rock. Just to be on the safe side, the British Army guarded the apes between 1915 and 1991. If all else fails, there is always the individual depicted on the island's 5p coin.

GREAT BARRINGTON

'Scrip' is essentially currency that only has value in the context of a particular community, company or group of companies. Usually taking the form of certificates, tokens or receipts, it is not legal tender but can certainly function as cash. Under American law, private groups are allowed to print paper scrip so long as the notes do not resemble US dollars. One New England town has decided to take advantage of this legal provision by adopting a currency of its own.

Great Barrington, Massachusetts (population 7,400) is a popular weekend retreat for New Yorkers of the New Age persuasion. Since 2006, they have been able to pay for their yoga lessons, chakra balancing sessions and cups of chai with either US dollars or 'BerkShares'. There is a significant advantage to using the latter, which are named after the nearby Berkshire Hills. The local currency is pegged to the dollar at a fixed exchange rate of one BerkShare to 90 cents, but businesses that subscribe to the scheme accept the two interchangeably. As a result, anyone paying in BerkShares effectively receives a 10% discount.

The scheme was set up by a non-profit organisation called the EF Schumacher Society with the aim of strengthening the local economy. People with BerkShares in their pockets are going to buy locally by definition and tourists are obviously attracted by the favourable exchange rate. The 10% discount may seem harsh on businesses that accept BerkShares but have to buy their supplies elsewhere in US dollars, but the hit they take tends to be more than offset by the resulting increase in trade. In any case, they always have the option of discreetly bumping up their prices to compensate.

As of June 2007 there were approximately 844,000 BerkShares in circulation with a combined value of $759,600. Obtaining BerkShares couldn't be easier. Several banks in the Great Barrington area are happy to exchange them for dollars at a rate of 10 to 9.

GREENLAND

Greenland is an autonomous province of Denmark and as such its currency is the Danish krone. Nevertheless, the vast Arctic island was issued with its own banknotes between 1803 and 1968 and its own coins from 1926 to 1964. In recent years Greenland has used regular Danish krone, but in 2006, the Copenhagen and Nuuk governments jointly announced that distinctive Greenlandic banknotes would be reintroduced by 2008. Judging by these exquisite examples from the 1950s and 1960s, this is something to look forward to.

HELL MONEY

These eight-billion-dollar notes are printed in Hong Kong, but intended for use in a rather different environment, namely the afterlife. Traditionally-minded Chinese people believe the best way to get them there is to burn them, which they do at two festivals: Yue Laan (Hungry Ghost Festival) and Ching Ming (Festival of Pure Brightness). The notes are destined for deceased relatives, who are presumed to require the same material goods as they did during their earthly lives. For this reason, paper models of cars, mobile phones, houses and anything else you care to mention are routinely burned alongside this 'Hell money'.

The fact that the Chinese call the kingdom of the hereafter 'Hell' should not be taken as a sign that they have a gloomy view of life beyond the grave. Indeed, the fact they believe their departed relatives will be able to find use for 10-figure notes in 'Hell' suggests they see it as a fairly jolly place. The explanation for the confusing nomenclature probably goes back to the days when Christian missionaries first went to China. When they warned the locals that they were heading for hell when they died, it would have been natural for them to assume that this was the Western word for 'afterlife'.

Hell money comes in various denominations, ranging from a few cents to the whopper. In addition to propitious symbols like carp and Fu dogs, the notes invariably feature portraits of the Lord of Hell. According to legend, he was once a living emperor who was awarded the post in recognition of his greatness on Earth.

HIGHEST DENOMINATION

This is the highest denomination banknote ever. Although never issued, it was printed in Hungary at the height of the country's hyperinflation crisis in 1946. This was a serious affair. The monthly inflation rate for July 1946, when prices doubled on average every 15 hours, was 41,900,000,000,000,000%. 'B-Pengo' stands for 'billion pengo', and that's the old European billion, equivalent to a trillion in the modern (American) system. A milliard, meanwhile, is 1,000 million, or what is now known as a billion. One milliard B-Pengo is therefore a billion trillion pengo. If written in full, this number would have

21 noughts. The Hungarian authorities recognised this would look a bit silly, so they expressed the note's value in words.

The highest denomination note actually issued during the crisis, and therefore in history, is shown below:

It was worth a pathetic 100 million B-Pengo, or 10^{18} of the little fellows. No wonder the woman in the headscarf looks a little sheepish. Nevertheless, the note still represented 40 billion pengo for every person alive on Earth at the time.

HOLOGRAMS

One of the best and most attractive ways to deter forgery is to stamp banknotes with holograms or other glittery images. Most of the so-called holograms on banknotes are actually Optically Variable Devices (OVDs). These are reflective designs etched into silver or gold foil that change colour according to the angle at which they are viewed. The first nation to use an OVD in a banknote was Australia. It consisted of a rather spooky image of Captain James Cook on the A$10 note issued to commemorate the 200th anniversary of his 'discovery' of the island. A cuter example is the camel motif found on this 1997 20 nakfa note from Eritrea:

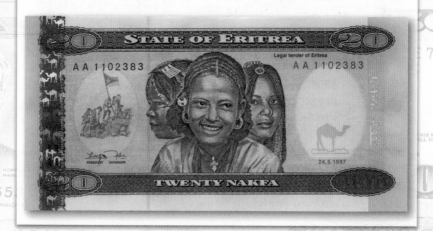

 Some notes, however, do contain genuine holograms. The defining feature of a holographic image is a convincing illusion of depth, and that certainly applies to the foil stamp embedded in the 20 dinar banknote issued by Bahrain in 1998 (pictured left).

It isn't easy to illustrate a hologram in a two-dimensional book, but you should be able to make out the head of an oryx (a large and beautiful antelope native to Bahrain) surrounded by 20s. In the real world, you would tend to see one or the other depending on the angle at which you were holding the note.

INDIA

The image of Mahatma Gandhi appears on all banknotes currently in circulation in India, but the 'zero rupees' note is particularly Gandhi-ish in spirit. The leader of the Indian independence movement was famed for the protest technique of passive resistance, and passive resistance is what this uniquely valueless piece of money is all about.

Corruption is rife in the subcontinent. A favoured way for an official to request a backhander is to ask Gandhi to 'smile' upon him. In 2007, an anti-corruption group called 5th Pillar decided to take this euphemism literally. It printed 25,000 zero rupees notes and distributed them to residents of the southern city of Chennai. Individuals and businesses were encouraged to hand them over when pressured to pay *baksheesh*. The bureaucrat in question would then either have to accept them or make an overt and therefore risky demand for cash.

Initial results have been encouraging. One rickshaw driver said he reduced a policeman to helpless giggles when he gave him one of the notes in response to a demand for cash. The officer had pulled him over and said that he would only release him if he was 'looked after'. The driver's audacity changed his mind.

As it clearly has no exchange value, the zero rupees note is not legal tender. Nevertheless, the Gandhi side is an almost direct copy of the one on the standard 50 rupee note. There are two main differences: the slogan 'Eliminate corruption at all levels' replaces the heading 'Reserve Bank of India', and the

Gandhi pictured on
a 500 rupee note

pledge reads 'I promise to neither accept nor give bribe' rather than 'I promise to pay the bearer the sum of fifty rupees'. It is the other side of the note that safeguards 5th Pillar against counterfeiting charges. In place of the Indian parliament building it features the organisation's mission statement.

✺

Only slightly more valuable than the Gandhi note above was the controversial 1 rupee coin issued to mark George V's succession to the British throne in 1911. On the head side, the king-emperor was depicted wearing the chain of the Order of the Indian Elephant. Unfortunately, the engraving was of such poor quality the eponymous pachyderm ended up looking more like a pig. As Islam regards pigs as unclean, India's Muslims were outraged. The Hindus, to whom elephants were sacred, weren't thrilled either. In the end, the coin had to be withdrawn and redesigned.

IRAN

In 2007, amid mounting international pressure to abandon its nuclear development programme, Iran issued a defiant 50,000 rial note. It features a cloud of orbiting electrons – a recognised nuclear symbol – accompanied by a *hadith* or saying of Prophet Mohammed that reads: 'If scientific knowledge exists as far away as the Pleiades [a constellation also known as The Seven Sisters], men from Persia will reach it.'

IRELAND

The Irish pound, punt, or if you want to be really technical, the Saorstát, came into existence in 1927. It ceased to be legal tender on 9 February 2002 when it was replaced by the euro. For much of its 75-year history, the punt was identical in value to the English pound, but the two currencies parted company in March 1979. This was a consequence of the Republic of Ireland joining the European Monetary System (ERM) and the UK deciding not to. Both countries decimalised on 15 February 1971, and prior to 2002, their notes and coins were issued in the same denominations. There was one glorious exception. The Irish retained a £100 note, an example of which the author was lucky enough to be given by mistake at the age of eight. It was handed over by an eccentric and shortsighted Irish cousin who thought he was giving him a tenner.

ISLE OF MAN

The Isle of Man, which is famous for its tailless felines, also issues special 'cat crowns'. The Manx pound, like its Scottish and Northern Irish equivalents, is a local issue of sterling rather than a separate currency. All the island's banknotes feature the three-legged symbol known as the Triskeles.

A different variety of puss is featured every year on the tails side (a somewhat ironic location for the Manx cat which began the series in 1988). Recent breeds to have appeared on the coins include the Long-haired Smoke (1997) and the Tonkinese (2004), but there is always a small Manx cat lurking somewhere in the background.

ITALY

If you wear a garment adorned with small, glittering metallic discs, you are inadvertently paying homage to the coin depicted above. For this is the original sequin, or *zecchino*, as it was known in its native Italy. First minted in Venice in 1284, it weighed about 3.5g and was 98.6% pure gold. The example shown is from the time of Antonio Venier, Doge of Venice from 1382-1400. The word *zecchino* is derived from *zecca*, the name of the Venetian mint. The coin was also known as the *ducat* as it was inscribed with the word *duca*, meaning duchy. The *ducat* remained an important trade currency in Europe until World War I.

IVORY COAST/
COTE D'IVOIRE

The strange image at the centre of this 2,000-franc note (2003) is a stylised sawfish. It represents a type of bronze figurine once used by the Akan people of the Ivory Coast to weigh gold dust. Up until the nineteenth century, gold was plentiful in the country's rivers (and in those of neighbouring Ghana, which used to be called the Gold Coast). The Akan traditionally regarded the sawfish as a symbol of prosperity and the authority of the king. As a result, using one to weigh gold was seen as highly appropriate. The sawfish device is also used as a watermark in the nation's banknotes.

The currency of the Ivory Coast has another claim to fame. In 1920, the then French colony issued the world's smallest banknotes. In response to a shortage of paper money, the authorities mounted 5, 10 and 25 centime postage stamps on pieces of cardboard and converted them into money. The 'notes' were overprinted with the words *valeur d'échange* ('exchange value') followed by 0.05, 0.10 and 0.25 francs respectively. They measured 32 x 46mm.

JAMAICA

The lady featured on this Jamaican banknote was called Nanny, but the cosy picture this conjures up couldn't be further removed from the truth. Rather than being a cuddly nursery maid, Nanny was a fearsome warrior. She was a charismatic leader of the Maroons, the runaway slaves who fought to drive the British from Jamaica during the eighteenth and nineteenth centuries.

MAHARISHI VEDIC CITY

Maharishi Mahesh Yogi is the inventor of Transcendental Meditation and a former guru of the Beatles. In 1991, a group of his followers purchased

3,000 acres (1,214ha) of land two miles (3.2km) to the north of Fairfield, Iowa, and set about building a town in accordance with the Maharishi's architectural teachings. Every edifice was orientated to the east and equipped with a central silent space plus a golden roof ornament called a *kalash*. The town was incorporated (officially recognised) on 21 July 2001. It was initially called Vedic City, but in November 2003 residents voted to add the word 'Maharishi'.

In February 2002, the city council introduced a new form of currency to Vedic City called the 'Raam Mudra'. The notes are printed in the Netherlands by the treasury arm of the Maharishi's 'Global Country of World Peace' organisation. The dollar/raam exchange rate is pegged at 10 to 1 and Vedic banknotes are available in three denominations: 1 raam (green), 5 raam (blue) and 10 raam (yellow/orange). They can be freely spent within the city, although customers are likely to receive their change in regular dollars.

The local currency is entirely legal. The Maharishis did their homework and a spokeswoman from the US Bureau of Engraving has said on record: 'If a merchant wants to accept the Raam, it's within their right to do so... as long as it's not classified as being lawful money or legal tender of this country.' But the Jefferson County Board of Supervisors has decreed that residents of Maharishi Vedic City must pay their bills in US currency.

Meanwhile, as Kim Pitts, the owner of a bookshop in Fairfield, has said: 'We don't know how it [the Raam Mudra] is backed. I mean, I guess I could print up Kim money if I wanted to.'

MEANINGS OF CURRENCY NAMES

The names of currencies often have interesting meanings or derivations:

CURRENCY	COUNTRY	MEANING
Birr	Ethiopia	'White thing' (from Amharic verb meaning 'to be white')
Cedi	Ghana	'Small shell' (Akan language)
Cruzeiro	Brazil	From Portuguese *cruz*, meaning 'a cross' (Cruzeiros were replaced by Reais in 1994)
Dobra	São Tomé (from Portuguese) and Príncipe	'Folding'
Escudo	Portugal	'Shield bearing coat of arms'
Gourde	Haiti	'Gourd' (a hollow plant pod used as receptacle)
Inti	Peru	'Sun' in Quechua language, referring to the Supreme god of the Incas (replaced by *Nuevos Soles*, or 'new suns')
Kina	Papua New Guinea	'Pearl shell' in Pidgin and Kuanua
Kopek (coin)	Russia, Ukraine, Belarus	Derived from word meaning 'spear'
Kuna	Croatia	'Marten' (the furs of these mammals were used as a currency in the Middle Ages)

Kwacha	Zambia	'Dawn' (Bemba language)
Kyat	Burma	'Round and flat'
Lari	Georgia	'Property' or 'hoard' (Old Georgian)
Leu/Lei	Romania, Moldova	'Lion(s)'
Lev(a)	Bulgaria	"
Nakfa	Eritrea	Name of town at centre of country's struggle for independence from Ethiopia
Pa'anga	Tonga	'Bean-shaped pieces'
Pataca	Macao	'Paw' (Portuguese)
Pengo (old coins)	Hungary	'Twang' (presumably referring to the sound the coins made when hitting something)
Pula	Botswana	'Rain' (Setswana language. Botswana is largely desert)
Quetzal	Guatemala	Name of a spectacular long-tailed rainforest bird
Riel	Cambodia	'One that shines'
Ringgit	Malaysia	'Jagged'
Rouble	Russia	Derived from verb *rubit*, meaning 'to cut up'
Som	Kyrghyzstan	'Pure'
Tambala (coins)	Malawi	'Cockerel' (Chewa language)
Zloty	Poland	'Golden'

MILLION-POUND NOTES

By law, Northern Irish and Scottish banknotes have to be backed pound for pound by Bank of England notes. As the sums in question run into the billions, it would be very cumbersome to use regular denominations for this purpose. Instead, the Bank uses special million-pound notes for its internal accounting.

MONGOLIA

Some nations would hesitate to place images of military leaders known for ruthlessness and butchery on their banknotes, but not the Mongolians. A portrait of Genghis Khan, or Chinggis Khan as his name is more accurately transliterated, has featured on almost all the Mongolian banknotes issued since 1997, including the 10,000 tugrik note shown below. On the few occasions when it hasn't, he has still sneaked in as a watermark.

Genghis Khan (1162-1227) was the founder of the largest contiguous empire in the history of the world. His fearsome reputation was well deserved – he slaughtered entire populations of cities that resisted him such as Herat and Merv – but he was also a brilliant military strategist. Above all, from the Mongolian point of view, he was responsible for uniting the nation and bringing it global fame. His countrymen regard him as having a similar or superior stature to Alexander the Great. In recent years in particular, as Mongolia has asserted itself after decades of Soviet control, he has become a symbol of national identity.

MOZAMBIQUE

The figures depicted on this 500 meticais note from Mozambique are some of the ugliest ever to feature on paper money. Neither of the characters on the left would stand much chance in a beauty contest, which is appropriate as they represent hunger. The figures on the right, however, have less excuse. They symbolise dance.

NORTHERN IRELAND

The Northern Irish monetary system makes Scotland's (qv) look positively simple, as there are four note-issuing banks as opposed to three. (It could be worse; 50 years ago there were eight.) As you will see, you have to have your wits about you when dealing with Northern Ireland pounds as the colours of a given denomination can vary substantially.

BANK OF IRELAND
All the Bank of Ireland notes have images of Queen's University, Belfast, on the front. The bank prints notes in four denominations: £5 (blue), £10 (pink), £20 (green) and £50 (blue green).

NORTHERN BANK
Aesthetically, the Northern Bank notes are probably the pick of the bunch. Tiresomely, from the bank's point of view, it had to recall all its notes following the theft of some £22 million from its Belfast money-handling centre in December 2004. The following spring they were reissued in new colours. They were also equipped with a new logo, which itself went out of date when the Bank was purchased by Danske Bank later in 2005.

Here is a summary of the Northern Bank notes with their old and new colours:

£5 (blue/blue)	This is an interesting note for three reasons. It is made of plastic, printed vertically rather than horizontally and it features an image of the space shuttle. Quite what this has to do with Northern Ireland is anyone's guess
£10 (green/brown)	Face – JB Dunlop (1840-1921), founder, Dunlop Tyres Reverse – the portico of Belfast City Hall
£20 (blue/purple)	Face – Harry Ferguson (1884-1960), tractor pioneer and the first Irishman to fly. Known as 'the mad mechanic' Reverse – the portico of Belfast City Hall
£50 (purple/blue)	Face – Sir Samuel Davison (1846-1921), inventor of tea-drying equipment and forward bladed centrifugal fan Reverse – the portico of Belfast City Hall
£100 (red/black)	Face – Sir James Martin (1893-1921), inventor of the aeroplane ejector seat Reverse – the portico of Belfast City Hall

FIRST TRUST BANK

The First Trust Bank was formed when the northern branches of the Allied Irish Bank merged with the TSB. Its banknotes feature generic Northern Irish folk on the front and scenes related to the Spanish Armada on the reverse.

| £10 (pinkish) | Face – a young man in a polo neck jumper |
| | Reverse – the sinking of the *Girona*, a Spanish ship that foundered at Lacada Point in September 1588 |

| £20 (pinkish) | Face – a middle-aged woman with a lacy collar |
| | Reverse – the chimney at Lacada Point, scene of the wreck of the *Girona* |

| £50 (blue-green) | Face – a middle-aged man in a suit and tie |
| | Reverse – old picture of the Spanish Armada inside a commemorative medal and held by a cherub |

| £100 (blue-green with a brown band) | Face – the characters from the fronts of the £20 and £50 notes side by side |
| | Reverse – another image of the Spanish Armada, this time without the medallion and cherub |

ULSTER BANK

With one glorious exception, Ulster banknotes are relatively subdued. The fronts depict the seafront at Belfast with a field of haystacks to the left and the Giant's Causeway on the right. The reverses have the bank's coat of arms.

The colours of the notes are: £5 (grey), £10 (blue-green), £20 (purple) and £50 (blue).

THE BEST FIVER EVER

The exception mentioned earlier is this £5 note issued by Ulster Bank in 2006 to mark the death of Northern Ireland football legend George Best, one of the greatest players of all time. The entire issue of one million special edition notes sold out within hours.

OLDEST BANKNOTE

Paper money was invented in China during the ninth century (see page 15). Appropriately enough, the world's oldest surviving banknote is also Chinese. It dates from the reign of Emperor Hongwu (1368-1398) and is printed on paper made from the mulberry tree. The six characters on the top mean 'Great Ming payable precious note'. The top half of the note's central panel states its value (1 kuan), illustrated by a depiction of 10 strings of 10 coins. The columns to either side repeat the 'Great Ming ⇒

payable precious note' message and add that it is 'payable everywhere'. The text in the lower half of the main panel read 'Ministry of Interior and Finance. Printed with the approval of the Emperor. Great Ming treasure note payable in copper cash. Users of counterfeits will be beheaded. Informers will be rewarded with 250 taels of silver in addition to the confiscated property of the convicted. Reign of Hongwu'.

When Marco Polo returned from his travels in 1295, he told fellow Europeans about the paper money used in China but nobody believed him.

OLDEST COIN

The title of the world's oldest coin is hotly disputed, but a Lydian one sixth of a stater piece owned by the British Museum is certainly a contender. Minted around 650-600BC, it was found in Ephesus in Turkey. It is made of electrum, a naturally occurring alloy of gold and silver that was once plentiful in Lydia's River Pactolus. Legend has it that it got there when King Midas, who was from neighbouring Phrygia, took a dip in the river in an attempt to wash away his curse, namely everything he touched turned to gold.

Incidentally but not coincidentally, the proverbially rich King Croesus was a Lydian. He ruled the country from around 560-546BC.

PALAU

In addition to providing the limestone for the stone money of Yap (see page 142), the tiny Pacific island republic of Palau has built a reputation for producing interesting examples of NCLT (Non Circulating Legal Tender). A silver $5 coin issued in 2006 is a case in point. It contains a tiny fragment of the so-called Nantan meteorite, a celestial lump of iron that landed in Guangxi province in China, in May 1516. According to a contemporary account, 'during summertime in May of Jiajing 11th year, stars fell from the northwest direction, five to six fold long, waving like snakes and dragons. They were as bright as lightning and disappeared in seconds'. Observations of iron meteorites in descent are as rare as hens' teeth.

Other numismatic novelties from Palau include a $5 coin studded with an authentic black pearl and another containing a genuine four-leaf clover.

PEOPLE APPEARING ON BANKNOTES OF MORE THAN ONE COUNTRY

With the exception of Queen Elizabeth II, which historical figure would you imagine has been depicted on the banknotes of the most countries? The answer is none other than Christopher Columbus, or Cristobal Colon, as he is known in the Spanish-speaking world. Aside from the fact that he 'discovered' the Americas, his popularity can be explained by the fact that the Spanish and Italians both claim him as one of their own. Portraits of CC have featured on notes of at least nine nations. In alphabetical order, they are:

Bahamas	$1 (1992)
Costa Rica*	Several denominations of old notes
Dominican Republic	500 pesos issued to commemorate 500th anniversary of Columbus's discovery of the Americas
El Salvador*	Almost every note issued since 1934
Italy	5,000 lire (1964-1970)
Nicaragua	Various old notes
Puerto Rico	$5 (1909)
Spain	Various pre-euro notes, including 5,000 pesetas (1992)
USA	$1,000 (1869-1880)

Christopher Columbus, pictured on the old 5,000 lire and 5,000 peseta banknotes

* The currencies of both Costa Rica and El Salvador are called the Colon (plural Colones) in honour of Columbus.

For good measure, Columbus also appears on the 2 euro coin issued by the Republic of San Marino to commemorate the 500th anniversary of the explorer's death.

✳

The man who comes second in the international banknote appearances chart is Simon Bolivar (1783-1830), the Venezuela-born leader of several nineteenth-century South

American independence movements. Bolivar has appeared on the notes of five nations: Bolivia (which is itself named after him), Colombia, Ecuador, Nicaragua and Venezuela.

In third place is Antonio José de Sucre, a comrade of Bolivar who also happened to be president of both Bolivia and Peru. He has made it onto the banknotes of four countries: Bolivia, Colombia, Ecuador and Venezuela.

Several people have appeared on the paper money of two countries. They include:

Marie Curie (Poland and France) – the discoverer of radium and the only non-royal woman to have gained the two currencies' honour.

Pedro Alvares Cabral (Portugal and Brazil) – leader of the Portuguese expedition that discovered Brazil.

Jozef Tito (Yugoslavia and Guinea) – for some reason Tito appealed to the Guinean leader Sékou Touré.

King Mohammed V (Morocco and Guinea) – Touré was also a fan of the Moroccan king.

José San Martín (Argentina and Uruguay) – another South American independence leader celebrated on banknotes on both sides of the Rio de la Plata.

THE PHILIPPINES

This 5 piso note from the 1970s is not as sinister as it may first appear. OK, it does depict a group of men clustered around a table with a skull on it, one of them is cutting himself with a knife and they are standing in front of a 'KKK' banner, but they have nothing to do with the Ku Klux Klan. Instead, the note commemorates the founding during the 1890s of the Katipunan Society (or, to give it its full name, Kataastaasan at Kagalanggalang Katipunan ng Mga Anak ng Bayan – 'The Highest and Most Honourable Society of the Sons of the Nation'). This underground organisation was at the forefront of the ultimately successful movement for independence from Spain.

PRINCIPALITY OF HUTT RIVER

The Principality of Hutt River is one of the world's more engaging micronations. Consisting of some 18,500 acres (7,487ha) of rolling farmland 370 miles (595km) north of Perth in Western Australia, it is ruled by a constitutional monarch and has a permanent population of around 30. It also has its own coins and banknotes.

The principality, or Hutt River Province as it was initially called, owes its existence to a bloody-minded farmer with an aptitude for law. In April 1970, Leonard Casley came up with an ingenious solution to a long-running dispute with the government of Western Australia over wheat quotas. He announced that his family farm was seceding from Australia. The bemused government decided not to respond. This was a fatal error. As Casley had discovered, Section 39 of the Western Australian penal code specified that anyone deemed to have 'infringed the integrity of the territory' had to be charged within two years or the case against the perpetrator would lapse. Accordingly, on 21 April 1972, the state government lost the legal right to challenge the new nation's declaration of independence.

A few months after the secession, a new Australian prime minister took office and announced that he was going to make a concerted effort to challenge Hutt River's self-proclaimed independence. To shore up the legal position of the province, Casley declared himself its prince, thus converting it into a principality. At the same time, and doubtless to her considerable relief, he pledged allegiance to Queen Elizabeth II. The net effect of these actions was to render anyone who would 'strike a blow' against the principality or its ruler guilty of treason under the Imperial Treasons Act of 1495.

Relations between the Principality and Australia have not always been good. In 1977 Prince Leonard went as far as declaring war on his larger neighbour, but fortunately no blood was shed. The Australian government has never recognised the mini-state (nor has any other country), but it has come to regard it as a legitimate business enterprise. Its economy is certainly in good shape. Prince Leonard and his wife Princess Shirley make an excellent living from tourism and the sale of Hutt River passports, postage stamps and currency. During their reign they have issued more than 200 coins commemorating everything from their diamond wedding anniversary to the supersaurus dinosaur.

SCOTLAND

Scotland currently has three note-issuing banks: the Bank of Scotland, The Royal Bank of Scotland and the Clydesdale Bank. As a consequence, the colours of the notes of a given denomination sometimes vary slightly, but not enough to cause serious confusion.

BANK OF SCOTLAND

The Bank of Scotland has found a neat solution to the question of who to depict on its banknotes. They all feature Sir Walter Scott (1771-1832), author of *Rob Roy*, *Ivanhoe* and several other classic historical novels.

The themes on the reverses of the Bank of Scotland notes are as follows:

£100 (red)	Leisure and tourism
£50 (green)	Arts and culture
£20 (pink)	Education and research
£10 (brown)	Distilling and brewing (no jokes please)
£5 (blue)	Oil and energy

THE ROYAL BANK OF SCOTLAND

The Royal Bank of Scotland is the only one of the three Scottish note-issuing banks to still print a £1 note. The numbers produced are dwindling as the pound coin increasingly takes over.

Like its similarly named competitor, The Royal Bank of Scotland sticks to using the portrait of one man on the front its banknotes, in this case Lord Ilay, the bank's first governor. The reverses are decorated with the following castles:

£100 (crimson)	Balmoral
£50 (green)	Inverness
£20 (purple)	Brodick
£10 (brown)	Glamis (pictured, home of a legendary 'monster')
£5 (blue)	Culzean
£1 (green)	Edinburgh

CLYDESDALE BANK

The Clydesdale bucks the trend by placing the image of a different famous Scot on each of its banknotes. The reverses are decorated with scenes connected to the characters on the fronts:

Denomination	Front	Reverse
£100 (red)	Lord Kelvin	Glasgow University
£50 (green)	Adam Smith	Industry against backdrop of sailing ships
£20 (pink)	Robert the Bruce	Robert the Bruce on horseback with Stirling Castle in the background
£10 (brown)	Mary Slessor	Missionary scenes, map of Calabar
£5 (blue)	Robert Burns	The rodent from his poem 'Ode to a Mouse'

COINS

Only the Royal Mint is entitled to issue Scottish coins. They are legal tender throughout the UK.

(NOT) LEGAL TENDER

As mentioned in the pound section (see page 20), Scottish banknotes, like their Northern Irish equivalents, are not legal tender. Instead, they are 'promissory notes'. 'Legal tender' is a somewhat technical term. It does not mean, as is often supposed, that the parties to a transaction are obliged to accept the notes and/or coins in question. It means that creditors are legally not allowed to reject them if they are offered as payment for debts. In practice, the question of whether or not a form of payment is legal tender is irrelevant to most transactions. Cheques and credit/debit cards aren't legal tender either, but tend to be accepted as people trust in them. The same is true of Scottish and Northern Irish banknotes, although the behaviour of certain English shopkeepers might suggest otherwise.

Bank of England notes are legal tender in England or Wales, but not in Scotland. Interestingly, in those countries the only denominations with that status are the £1 and £2 coins.

See pages 110 and 113 for the Northern Ireland entry and for a stimulating discussion of million-pound notes and their relevance to Scottish currency.

SEYCHELLES

Have a look at the two palm trees to the right of the Queen's portrait on this note from the Seychelles. They spell out the word 'sex', do they not? For this reason, the notes, issued between 1968 and 1973, have become eminently collectible. It would be interesting to psychoanalyse the designer. History does not record whether Her Majesty was amused.

SOMALIA

Somalia has existed in a state of anarchy since the early 1990s, with various factions and warlords fighting for control. In recent times, the closest thing the troubled east African nation has had to a government is the 'Transitional Federal Government of the Somali Republic' (TFG), a United Nations-backed body formed in Kenya in 2004. With the help of Ethiopian troops, the TFG managed to wrest control of the Somali capital Mogadishu from the Union of Islamic Courts (UIC) at the end of 2006.

To raise much-needed revenue, the TFG has taken to issuing colourful and bizarrely shaped coins designed to appeal to foreign collectors. The guitar varieties shown left, which are nominally valued at $1, have proved particularly popular. They are examples of what is known as non-circulating legal tender, ie forms of currency that are theoretically legitimate, but intended as souvenirs. We wouldn't advise anyone to try to test their validity in Somalia. For one thing, it is one of the most dangerous countries on Earth. For another, the locals, who are accustomed to dealing in Somali shillings, might be a bit nonplussed.

The six coins include: the Stratocaster Guitar Coin, the Flying 'V' Guitar Coin, the Gibson X-plorer Guitar Coin, the Klein Guitar Coin, the Stars and Stripes Guitar Coin and, rather oddly, the Gary Glitter Guitar Coin.

TATARSTAN

Tatarstan is a republic of the Russian Federation bounded by the Volga river to the west and the Ural mountains to the east. Just over half its four million people are Kazan Tartars, descendants of one of the Turkic tribes that fought alongside Attila the Hun. In the seventh century, the region that is now Tatarstan was home to the Kingdom of Great Bulgaria. Following the death of its ruler Kubrat Han, a chunk of the population migrated almost 1,500 miles (2,414km) to the site of modern Bulgaria. The rest stayed behind.

In 1552, Ivan the Terrible conquered Tatarstan and incorporated it into Russia. It remained part of the Russian Empire and then the USSR for 438 years, but in 1990 Tatarstan took advantage of the collapse of the Soviet Union to declare itself a sovereign state. Independence was short-lived – four years later Tatarstan became part of the Russian Federation – but in the meantime the government issued some highly unusual banknotes (or more properly currency cheques). They were printed without denominations. The rather stylish note (pictured left), for example, is a 100 rouble note from 1991, but you could spend a lifetime searching for a clue to its value. This startling omission was probably a reaction to the inflation that was bedevilling the republics of the former Soviet Union at the time. Rather than printing new notes every time the existing ones became virtually worthless, the Tatars decided to save time and money by retaining one set of notes and changing their nominal values if required.

TURKMENISTAN

There is something unusual about the 1 manat note from 1993 overleaf. It doesn't bear the portrait of Saparmurat Niyazov, Turkmenistan's president from 1990 to his death in 2006. Niyazov, or 'Turkmenbashi' ('Father of all Turkmen') as he had his parliament declare him in 1993, orchestrated a personality cult that would have made Chairman Mao blush. Among his most egregious excesses were naming a Caspian Sea port after himself, elevating the book of his political thoughts to the status of the Koran and constructing

136 MINTED

a 120-foot-high gold-plated statue of himself that rotated to follow the sun (brave locals joked it was the other way round). He even renamed months of the year in his honour. January became *Turkmenbashi* and April *Gurbansoltan Edzhe* to commemorate his mother.

By 1995, Niyazov had spotted his omission. His face appeared on every note and coin issued in that year and up to the time of his death.

WALES

England and Wales are considered one unit as far as cash is concerned, but although the principality does not have a currency of its own, it is home to the Royal Mint. In the late 1960s, it became apparent that the Mint's ancient home on Tower Hill in London was not up to the task of striking hundreds of millions of new coins in preparation for decimalisation in 1971. The decision was therefore taken to move the facility to Llantrisant, 10 miles (16km) to the west of Cardiff. The Queen opened the first phase of the new Mint on 17 December 1968.

Wales is represented on just one denomination of British currency, namely the £1 coin. The design on the reverse of the coins is changed every year in a five-year cycle, representing in turn the UK, Scotland, Wales, Northern Ireland and England. To date, the 'Welsh' years and images used have been as follows:

1985	A leek encircled by a coronet. The edge of the coin is inscribed with the words *Pleidiol Wyf I'm Gwlad* ('True am I to my country'), taken from the Welsh National Anthem
1990	As 1985
1995	Welsh dragon with *Pleidiol Wyf I'm Gwlad* inscription on the edge
2000	As 1995
2005	Menai suspension bridge. The edge is decorated with two overlapping lines, one curved and one angular

THE CHIEF TREASURY OF WALES AND THE BLACK SHEEP BANK

The fact that Wales is the only part of the UK to lack a banknote-issuing authority has long rankled with many of its inhabitants. During the late 1960s, the attempts of one Welshman to redress this situation attracted much public attention and an equal amount of amusement. Richard Williams from Llandudno was an Associate of the Institute of Bankers with a touch of the Leonard Casleys about him (see Principality of Hutt River on page 124). For three years, he ran rings around the British Board of Trade, which for a time seemed powerless to prevent him creating a separate Welsh currency.

The saga began in 1968, when Williams wrote to the British Prime Minister Harold Wilson to suggest the establishment of a 'Bank of Wales' to promote the Welsh economy. He received a reply from the Board of Trade to the effect that no company would be permitted to use that name unless it could prove that it deserved it. Williams responded with a formidable weapon – the Welsh language. He formed a company with a share capital of £100 split between himself and his wife and applied to register it in the name of 'Prif Trysorfa Cymru Limited'. The Board of Trade, blissfully unaware that this phrase meant 'Chief Treasury of Wales Limited', duly approved the application.

Williams' next step was to issue some currency. As a former banker, he knew he would get into legal hot water if he attempted to create a rival legal tender, so he began by issuing 'payment orders'. These worked in much the same way as cheques and could be used to pay bills and transfer funds. Williams knew enough about the clearing system to equip each payment order with a block of black ink in which the data the banking system needed to process the orders could be included.

In 1969, the Board of Trade, which had finally worked out the meaning of *Prif Trysorfa Cymru*, wrote to Williams asking if he might like to change the company's name. He replied that he would not and added he was about to up the stakes by issuing promissory notes payable on demand. To test the waters, he banged out four such notes on his typewriter, one for 10 shillings, one for £1, one for £5 and one for £10. Each stated in Welsh that the Chief Treasury of Wales promised to pay the bearer the relevant sum on demand. To validate the notes, he needed them to carry two-penny duty stamps from the Board of the Inland Revenue, so he posted them to the revenue, which obliged without a squeak.

Emboldened, Williams printed several more notes, decorating the fronts with a red Welsh dragon astride an abacus and the reverses with a reproduction of a Victorian watercolour of Caernarvon Castle that happened to hang in his house. Then he sent them to London to be stamped. Two hundred and one of the promissory notes were returned with the necessary revenue stamps. Their denominations were 10 shillings (100), £1 (49), £5 and £10 (26 each). They are now valuable collectors items.

By the time Williams sent the next batch of notes to be stamped, the authorities had started to wise up, not least because of the media attention the case had begun to generate. The Board of the Inland Revenue returned the consignment, pointing out promissory notes with a value of less than £5 could not be issued under the terms of the 1826 Bank Notes Act. Taking the Board at its word, Williams resent the notes worth £5 and above. They were returned duly stamped.

At this point, the Board of Trade decided to renew its efforts to halt Richard Williams' project. In March 1969, it wrote a letter ordering him to change the name of his company. When he proposed the new moniker 'Cwmni y Ddafad Ddu Gymreig Limited', the board approved its registration. The revised title meant 'Welsh Black Sheep Company'. This had been the colloquial name for the last independent Welsh bank, the Aberystwyth and Tregaron. As every Welshman knew, this institution was famous for printing its notes with the number of black sheep that corresponded to their denominations. Williams elaborated on this example, decorating his new 10-shilling note with a black lamb, the £1 note with a ewe, the £5 with a ram and the £10 with two rams.

The Welsh Black Sheep Company continued to print notes for two years, bowing out with a decimal issue in 1971. By this stage Williams had proved his point.

YAP

Overleaf is an example of the legendary stone money of the Micronesian island of Yap. Try walking around with a few of these in your pocket...

The story of the *rai* coins, as they are known, begins several hundred years ago. One day, a group of Yapese fishermen found themselves lost at sea some 250 miles from home. Eventually, they steered their outrigger canoe to the island of Palau, home to distinctive outcrops of limestone with which the men were much taken. They decided to break off a chunk of the rock, decorate it with carvings made with shell tools and take it home as a souvenir. It was shaped like a whale, or *rai* in their language. When the fishermen returned to Yap with this novel item, the locals were mighty impressed.

The episode coincided with a power struggle among local chiefs in which the key issue was status. It was immediately agreed the *rai* was the most desirable object on the island. Its possession gave enormous kudos to the clan whose members had brought it to Yap. As a result, rival factions began to dispatch canoes to Palau to obtain *rai* of their own. To facilitate transportation, they simplified the standard design to a disc with a hole in the middle. By passing a beam through the hole, even the biggest *rai* could be rendered relatively easy to carry. And some of them were seriously big. The largest were 12 feet (3.7m) in diameter and weighed several tons.

Prior to the *rai* revolution, the people of Yap had conducted transactions using commodities like rare shells and turmeric, but the stones soon took over as the primary currency. They were valued according to several criteria. The most important was the number of lives lost in the process of obtaining them from Palau. Next came the quality of the carving and then the identity (if any) of the chief who had sponsored the quarrying trip. Size also mattered, but a small, beautifully carved stone acquired on a journey with many fatalities commissioned by a great chief could easily be worth more than one considerably larger.

The portability problem was solved in various ways. Stones planted outside private dwellings tended to belong to the owner, while those erected in public places such as dancing grounds could only be exchanged through elaborate ceremonies attended by the entire community. There was therefore little danger of anyone forgetting which *rai* belonged to whom.

The people of Yap managed their *rai*-based economy remarkably well prior to the nineteenth century, but the system was ruined by an Irish American called David O'Keefe. After being shipwrecked off the island during the 1870s, he saw an opportunity to make a fortune by exploiting the local demand for the giant stone discs. Using modern nautical and stonecutting techniques, he began to import them from Palau by the shipload. The upshot was rampant inflation and a debasement of value.

Rai stones are still treasured by the people of Yap, but are no longer regularly used as money. The younger generation shows a preference for the US dollar.

ZAMBIA

To commemorate the 2000 Olympics in Sydney, Australia, Zambia issued a 5,000 kwacha coin that demonstrated the bonds between the two countries in the most graphic way possible. It simply mashed their outlines together. This required the relative size of Zambia to be exaggerated approximately tenfold. On the whole the shapes of Zambia and Australia jigsawed together quite nicely, but to secure a perfect fit it was necessary to incorporate the Gulf of Carpentaria and a fair chunk of the Arafura Sea.

UNUSUAL DENOMINATIONS

The banknotes and coins below make a refreshing change from the denominational norms of singles, fives, tens, twenties and so on.

CANADA

According to www.urbandictionary.com, to 'slip a $4 bill' is to tell a person a lie to get them to do something they ordinarily wouldn't. The phrase is thus related to the British expression 'as bent as a nine-bob note', ie totally crooked. Yet despite the proverbial implausibility of such banknotes, $4 bills really did once exist. Between 1871 and 1912, they were legal tender in the Dominion of Canada (the British portion of the territory during the colonial era). The fellow with the moustache in the below example from 1882 is the Marques of Lorne, later the 9th Duke of Argyll. He was Governor General of the Dominion from 1878-1883.

JERSEY

The Channel Islands, of which Jersey is the largest, are owned by Britain but lie much closer to France. British and French currencies were both used on the island prior to 1834, but in that year an act of parliament made sterling the sole legal tender. At the time, £1 was worth 26 livres. To put it another way, one shilling ($1/20$ of a pound) was worth 26 sous ($1/20$ of a livre). This placed islanders accustomed to trading in sous in a numerical dilemma. The old 'Jersey Penny' (two sous) was suddenly $1/13$ of a shilling. In the same vein, the Jersey ha' penny was now $1/26$ of a shilling and the farthing $1/52$. Rather than force locals to abandon their old accounting system, the Royal Mint elected to provide them with denominations they could relate to. In 1841, three new coins were struck, worth $1/13$, $1/26$ and $1/52$ of a shilling respectively. Thirty-one years later, Jersey finally adopted the English system of 12 pennies to the shilling, whereupon the coins were withdrawn.

148 MINTED

BURMA

Burma's military dictator Ne Win had a thing about numbers. In 1985, he demonetised the country's 50 and 100 kyat banknotes and replaced them with notes in three less-than-obvious denominations: 15, 35 and 75 kyats. The change was ostensibly made to counter black-market activity, but many interpreted it as a reflection of Ne Win's taste for numerology. The 75 kyat note, for example, was issued to coincide with his 75th birthday.

Two years later, Ne Win cancelled the new denominations without warning, rendering 75% of the country's banknotes obsolete overnight. The reason for this rather drastic move was the dictator's growing fondness for the number nine. Noting the digits in 45 and 90 kyats added up to his favourite number, he printed reams of notes in these denominations to replace the abandoned versions. The economic consequences of Ne Win's whim precipitated serious riots and ultimately the coup that ousted him in 1988.

Left: Burma's Ne Win pictured
on the country's 35 kyat and
5 kyat banknotes

150 MINTED

Money, it's a gas.
Grab that cash with both hands
and make a stash

— Pink Floyd, 'Money'

BIBLIOGRAPHY

As banknotes and coins are a) an important part of almost everyone's life and b) avidly collected by millions of people worldwide, there is no shortage of good material out there. Here are just a few of the sources that the author has found useful:

Standard Catalog of World Paper Money, Volume 2, General Issues 1368-1960 (11th revised edition) – Edited by George S Cuhaj
Standard Catalog of World Paper Money, Volume 3, Modern Issues (13th revised edition) – George S Cuhaj
The World Encyclopedia of Coins and Coin Collecting – James Mackay
www.banknotes.com
www.ibns.it – the International Banknote Society
www.bankofengland.co.uk
www.moneyfactory.com – the US Bureau of Engraving and Printing
www.pjsymes.com.au – a prolific writer on world currencies
www.tomchao.com – a collector with an eye for a good story

ILLUSTRATIONS

The publishers would like to thank the following for their invaluable help with images: Audrius Tomonis at banknotes.com, www.chards.co.uk, www.joelscoins.com, Tom Chao, Bruce Lorich, Mary Evans Picture Library, and Ken Elks.

Lack of money is the root of all evil

– George Bernard Shaw